ISBN: 979-8-9934848-2-2
Cover and interior design by Maylene Peña
Published by Levi Group LLC
www.levigroupllc.com
Chicago, Illinois

For more information, visit:
www.maylenepena.com

Printed in the United States of America
First Edition – 2026

Written in surrender.

Carried by grace.

Released in faith.

May every heart that touches these pages find itself held by God.

To El Roi,
the God who saw me in the wilderness and stayed.
You held me together when the pieces of my life felt too shattered to gather.
You called even the broken places SACRED.

To Rafael,
thank you for being the place where my heart could finally exhale.
We walked into love, steady and unhurried.
Your love is shelter, not weight.
Home, not demand.
Rest, not performance.

To our children, Jelani, Jelise and Jeliel,
you are the reason I will always keep becoming.
Loving you grows me, stretches me, strips me, and rebuilds me.
You teach me that motherhood is both altar and inheritance.
Everything I am becoming is for God,
but much of who I will become, I learn through you every day along the way. *My biggest flex is being your Momma.* <3

To my sisters, and my brothers,
the ones who share my blood and remember my beginnings,
and the ones who chose me without needing history to justify love.
You held me through the breaking and the rebuilding.
Your love and support are stitched into my story. This Story.

To my parents, Carlos and Angela Chica,
the ones who birthed me in their hearts and midwifed my calling; thank you for covering me, correcting me, and calling me into wholeness.
Your obedience created a pathway I could walk with courage.
Your faith shaped my faith.
Your yes made room for mine.

And to the woman who is still becoming,
may you know that the mess does not disqualify you.
It is where God meets you, forms you, strengthens you,
and teaches you how to rise again.
You are not becoming alone.

Are you Ready?

Prologue
How did we get here?

[8] We are hard pressed on every side, but not crushed; perplexed, but not in despair; [9] persecuted, but not abandoned; struck down, but not destroyed."

— 2 Corinthians 4:8-9

There was a moment; not dramatic, not loud, but *heavy* in a way only a woman carrying too much can understand.

The house was not quiet, but it felt lonely, nonetheless.

Life was doing its thing. Someone needed something. Someone always needs something. Dinner still wasn't figured out. Dinner is never figured out. And despite being silent for the last 8 years, my phone kept lighting up with responsibilities that never care how tired I was.

And somewhere in the middle of being a wife, a mother, and a leader… I realized something uncomfortable:

I did not know where I ended and everything else began.

I love my husband.
I love my children.
I love the call of God on my life.

But love did not cancel the weight; It still feels heavy.

There were days when I moved from one role to the next so seamlessly that no one noticed I was disappearing in the process.

Smiling. Serving. Showing up.

And still wondering quietly:
"Why does this feel so hard if I'm doing what God asked me to do?"

No one really prepares you for this part.

They celebrate your "yes." They affirm your strength.
They call you resilient, capable, anointed, chosen.

But they rarely talk about what it feels like to live inside that yes when it stretches you past what feels sustainable. When you cannot possible listen to another living soul call you "the strongest person they know" without wanting to scream.

Marriage will ask you to love when you are tired.
Motherhood will ask you to give when you feel empty.
Ministry will ask you to pour when no one sees the cost.

And somewhere in between all of that, you will come face to face with yourself.

Not the polished version. Not the strong version. Not the one everyone applauds.

The real one.

The one still healing. Still learning. Still a mess, but the mess that shows up every day to try again. **And there is nowhere to hide.**

This book was not written from a place of arrival. It was written from the middle.

From prayers whispered while folding laundry, or in my case, staring at the growing pile of clean clothes I still haven't folded.

From tears that fell quietly so no one would ask questions.
From moments where I had to choose, again and again,
to believe that God was still present
even when I felt stretched beyond recognition.

Because here is what I have learned:

God does not wait for you to get it together before He meets you.

He meets you in it.

In the tension. In the exhaustion.
In the in-between version of who you were and who you are becoming.

And if you stay there long enough, if you stop running from the mess and start letting Him work inside of it... you begin to see something unexpected:

The mess is not where you are falling apart.

It is where you are being formed.

And that is where this story begins.

Introduction

So, Press on Here

Even If You're Still Healing
Even If You're Still Figuring It Out

You are allowed to arrive here unfinished.
You are allowed to arrive here tired.
You are allowed to arrive here holding joy in one hand
and disappointment in the other.

God does not wait for you to be whole
before He begins to heal you.

This is not the end of your story.
This is the sacred beginning you could not yet see.

This is not a book about doing marriage, motherhood, and ministry *well.*

It is a book about living them **honestly.**

About the mornings when love feels like worship, when the days take turns, being endless and entirely short at the same time, and the nights when it all feels like work.

About being held by God using the hands of the most amazing humans, while holding babies, and callings at the same time, and realizing all three require a strength you do not have apart from God.

This book is for the woman who has ever thought:
"I should have figured this out by now."
The woman who is building a life in real time
with joy in one hand and exhaustion in the other.

For the wife who is still learning how to love without losing herself.
For the mother who is raising children while still raising the little girl inside herself.
For the leader who pours out and pours out... and sometimes forgets she is allowed to be filled, too.

This book does not promise ease. But it does promise this:

God is already in your mess.

Not waiting for you to arrive healed, disciplined, aligned, whole —
but present *right where the tears dried last.*

He is forming something holy out of every tension:
The marriage you are nurturing.
The children you are stewarding.
The calling you are carrying.

This is an invitation to stop striving for the polished version of yourself and instead — to lean into the sacred reality
that becoming is messy.

But it is also beautiful.

And you are not becoming alone.

Part One - Marriage

Chapter 1

The Foundation

Building a Christ-Centered Marriage

"Therefore, I will allure her into the wilderness and speak tenderly to her there."

— Hosea 2:14

Before Rafael, there was a wilderness.

Not the poetic kind.
Not the peaceful kind.
The kind where loneliness echoes.
Where healing feels like heartbreak.
Where God asks you to stay still
when everything in you wants to run.

Before Rafael, there were seven years of singleness. Seven years of raising my children, rebuilding my life after brokenness, and letting God deal with the parts of me I had learned to survive with but had never actually healed. Rafael was not my first husband, and our family is beautifully blended, but before I could enter a new covenant, I had to let God tell the truth about the old pain.

There were nights when I cried myself to sleep, asking God why love had broken me the way it did. There were days I parented through exhaustion, holding my babies close while feeling like no one was holding me. There were Sundays where I led worship with fire in my voice, but ashes in my chest.

In that season, I wore a gold wedding band. Not because I was pretending, but because I needed the reminder that I still belonged to God. Even after failure. Even after heartbreak. Even after the kind of disappointment that makes you question your own discernment. Divorce. That ring reminded me that I was not abandoned. I was still His, and if love ever came again, it would not come to complete me. It would come to complement what God had already been restoring.

Healing is not glamorous.
Becoming requires a letting go that feels like death.
Before I could love again, something in me had to die:

The version of me that believed I needed to perform to be chosen.
The version of me that accepted crumbs and called it covenant.
The version of me that thought love meant endurance without reciprocity.

The wilderness was where God unmade me.

Not to diminish me,
but to **restore me**.

He stripped away the parts of me that love had wounded,
and He healed me in ways I didn't realize I needed.

I thought I was waiting for a husband.
But I was being **rebuilt for covenant**.

And when Rafael came,
I didn't fall in love.
I *walked* into it… steady, whole, unhurried.

Because I was no longer starving.

The Moment Love Arrived

There was no whirlwind.
No dizzying rush.
No emotional firestorm that felt like destiny.

I had lived that kind of love before;
the kind that sweeps you up quick
and drops you even quicker.

This love was different.

We **walked** into love…
slowly, steadily, intentionally.
Eyes open. Hearts whole. No hiding. No performing.

I do not believe in better halves. I do not believe another person
completes what only God can fill. Rafael did not come into my life to
make me whole. He came as a partner who complemented the woman
God had already been healing.

When Rafael came, I did not fall in love. I walked into it; whole and
unhurried.

There was a softness to Rafael that I did not know how to trust at first
because it was terrifying.
Not because he was untrustworthy, but because I had never known
love that did not require endurance.

But he loved me without demanding anything from me.
He loved me like someone who knew where his love came from.

He did not rush me. He did not try to fix me.
He did not need me to prove I was worthy of being loved.

He just *showed up*.

Every day. Every season. Every small moment that makes a life.

And somewhere along the way — his presence became a place.

His hands became home.

Not the kind of home that locks you in,
but the kind that opens your chest
and lets you breathe.

A home where love doesn't devour, it **holds**.
A home where safety is not silent, it is **felt**.
A home where covenant is not performance, it is **rest**.

If the wilderness taught me how to be whole,
Rafael taught me that wholeness can be received.

He is my safe.
Not because he is perfect,
but because he is surrendered.

His heart is anchored in God.
And mine rests there too.

"Place me like a seal over your heart... for love is as strong as death."
— Song of Solomon 8:6

"Perfect love drives out fear."
— 1 John 4:18

This is not perfect love because we are perfect.
It is perfect because it is surrendered.

The Spiritual Truth

Love didn't come to rescue me.
It came because I was finally ready to be held. Covenant began when I was no longer starving for love.

Healing made space for love to be gentle.

God will never bring you into covenant from a place of desperation.

Desperation chooses anyone. Healing chooses well.

"Above all else, guard your heart, for everything you do flows from it."
— Proverbs 4:23

The wilderness was not punishment. It was preservation.

God needed to get me to a place where love was **a choice**, not a rescue.

So that when love came, I recognized it.
Received it. And did not run from it.

The Becoming

You may not be in the wilderness now...
or maybe you are.

But ask gently:

What part of me is still healing?

_____

_____

_____

_____

What have I learned to survive that God now wants to soften?

_____

_____

_____

_____

Where have I confused endurance with love?

_____

_____

_____

_____

You do not have to answer quickly.
Let the questions **sit** with you.

The wilderness is where God teaches us to hear our own souls again.

The Practice: Spiritual Inventory

A lot of us know how to make lists of what we want in a husband. We know how to pray for qualities, ask for confirmation, and hope for someone who loves God and loves us well. But before I made any list of what I wanted, I had to tell the truth about what I was bringing. I took inventory. Not of my preferences, but of my formation. Not of what I wanted to receive, but of what I was prepared to offer.

"Search me, O God, and know my heart; test me and know my anxious thoughts."
— Psalm 139:23

Take a breath.
There is no failing here.
Only *seeing*; and God meets us in truth.

Read slowly. Answer gently. Let your heart speak.

- Am I patient with the people I love, or do I rush them to become who I need them to be?
- Do I practice kindness when I am tired, frustrated, or unseen?
- Do I let resentment linger?
- Is God the center from which I love, or only the place I return to after I have tried everything else?
- Am I spiritually nourished, or am I pouring from emptiness?
- Do I listen to understand, or only to respond?
- Can I acknowledge when I am wrong without defending myself first?
- Am I building a life with my spouse, or simply living beside them?

Pause Here

If any question felt tender, make sure you write down your thoughts. There is something God wants to speak into that place.

Your tenderness is not weakness,
it is where God breathes.

Breath-Prayer After the Inventory

Lord, show me the places in me still learning how to love.
Not so that I may feel shame, but so that I may be free.
Soften every hardened place. Strengthen every weary place.
Make me whole in Your love again.

Lord, thank You for the wilderness that did not break me.
Thank You for the parts of me You healed quietly,
in the seasons no one saw.

Teach me to love from my wholeness,
not my wounds.

If there is anything in me still holding on to old versions of myself,
help me release them now.

Make my heart soft again.

Amen.

The Rhythm of Us

"His mercies are new every morning."

— Lamentations 3:22–23
Love has to be renewed, not assumed.

Marriage is not sustained by a single vow spoken once.
It is sustained by a thousand small yeses whispered across seasons.

Love is a **garden**, yes; full of things planted deliberately and things that bloom on their own.

But it is also a **dance**; requiring awareness, surrender, timing,
and the humility to be led and the courage to lead when the time is yours.

Some days the rhythm is effortless; steps matching steps,
breaths falling into harmony, love unfolding like sunlight on something blooming.

Other days require **re-learning each other**, reacquainting yourself with what hurts, what heals, what has changed and choosing them over and over.

Love does not stay the same, because *we* do not stay the same.

And this is not failure. This is life.

This is covenant.

Love does not rescue us from the wilderness; it meets us on the other side. Covenant is not found. It is recognized when the soul has healed enough to receive it. This is where love began for me; whole, unhurried, and holy.

The Garden

There are parts of love you must **tend**:

- gentleness
- gratitude
- affection
- presence

These must be watered. Not once. Not occasionally.
Regularly. Patiently.
Even when you don't see growth yet.

"Let us not become weary in doing good…"
— Galatians 6:9

Growth is happening even when you cannot see it.

The Dance

There are parts of love you must **choose**:

- to stay present when hurt wants to withdraw
- to listen when your pride wants to speak
- to soften when your ego wants to defend
- to try again after misunderstanding

"Make every effort to keep the unity of the Spirit through the bond of peace."
— Ephesians 4:3

Unity is not found. Unity is **kept**.

The Balance

Love lives in the space between:

Tending and choosing.
Softness and strength.
Grace and accountability.
Comfort and growth.

Marriage is not about perfect balance every day. It is about **returning to balance** when life tilts. And returning is holy.

The Grace Journal

This is not homework.
This is a **way of seeing again.**

Once a week (not daily, not forcing, just tending), ask:

Where did I see grace in us this week?

_____

_____

_____

Where did we move well together?

_____

_____

_____

*Where did we step on each other's feet and how can we soften
tomorrow?*

_____

_____

_____

Write **one sentence** of gratitude. Not five. Not paragraphs. Just one.

Because gardens grow from small things.
And dances are remembered one step at a time.

Reflection Pause

When has your marriage felt like a dance?

_____

_____

_____

When has it felt like a garden?

_____

_____

_____

What part of your marriage needs watering?

_____

_____

_____

Where do you feel the rhythm shifting and what is it inviting you to notice?

_____

_____

_____

Pause.

Let the answers come softly.

Simple Breath Prayer

God, teach us the rhythm of us.
Help us tend gently.
Help us choose willingly.
Let our love be a garden that grows and a dance that continues.
Amen.

What prayer is God whispering to your heart?

_____

_____

_____

_____

_____

_____

_____

_____

_____

_____

_____

_____

_____

Selah

Pause here.
Let your heart take a breath.

"Sometimes love doesn't come riding in;
it comes quietly, building altars in the ordinary."

Chapter 2

Fidelity & Forgiveness

When Love Becomes a Choice, not a Feeling

"Be kind and compassionate to one another, forgiving each other, just as in Christ God forgave you."

— Ephesians 4:32

Before I could understand covenant,
I had to survive counterfeit love.

There was a time when betrayal wasn't just a word
it was the only room I lived in. I know what it's like to love someone
who keeps their promises in public and breaks them in private.
To forgive until forgiveness feels like self-betrayal. To pray that
faithfulness will come while quietly grieving the pieces of yourself that
died waiting.

Somewhere along the way, I had to relearn what fidelity actually meant.

Fidelity is more than sexual exclusivity. It is loyalty in thought,
attention, affection, and intention. It is the daily protection of what
belongs inside the covenant.

I was cheated on in ways that left my heart fragmented. Each act of
infidelity didn't just break trust, it rewrote what I believed about love,
about worth, about God. And when the breaking kept coming,
something in me hardened. I told myself fidelity didn't matter
anymore. I mistook numbness for healing and rebellion for freedom.

There were seasons I gave pieces of myself away because I didn't
believe I was worth keeping whole. I forgave for the sake of forgiving,
but my forgiveness had no roots, it was survival dressed as strength.
Underneath it, bitterness grew quietly, and I carried shame like a secret
I didn't know how to confess.

But even in the ruins, God was rewriting the definition of faithfulness.
He wasn't asking me to hold a man together; He was holding *me.*

When Rafael came, I didn't know how to receive the kind of love that
didn't require me to beg. He was gentle where I expected punishment,
consistent where I braced for chaos. He didn't try to fix me;
he gave me room to heal with no judgement, just space as he gently
wiped my tears along the way.

And through him,
I began to see what covenant actually looks like.

Not perfection, but presence.
Not performance, but peace.

When rooted in safety, love becomes a choice, not a feeling.
I don't wake up every morning and decide *if* I love Rafael.
I made that decision once—at the altar—and I live it out daily.
Sometimes it looks like patience, sometimes it looks like laughter,
and sometimes it looks like silence that still feels like home.

Fidelity stopped being a command I had failed to keep
and became a reflection of the God who had never left me.
Forgiveness became the language of my healing,
not just toward the men who broke me,
but toward the woman I was when I stopped believing she was worth
faithfulness.

The Covenant We Keep

Marriage is a covenant; holy, weighty, and alive.
It is the echo of God's faithfulness to His people,
a reflection of His mercy that renews morning after morning.

Fidelity and forgiveness are its twin pillars. One sustains love; the other
redeems it. Together, they make room for grace to dwell between two
imperfect hearts.

Faithfulness is more than the absence of betrayal.
It is loyalty of thought, integrity of heart, and the steady choosing of
one another when emotions shift and storms roll in.

Forgiveness is not a single act. It is a rhythm… the daily washing of the
heartso that love remains free from resentment's residue.

Loving Rafael in His Natural Form

One of the most sacred lessons I have learned in marriage
is how to love Rafael as he is; every part of him as God intended,
not as I might imagine or wish him to be.

There was a time when I thought love meant shaping each other into better versions of ourselves— that pointing out flaws could somehow perfect us.

But love is not a project. And Rafael is not mine to fix.
Only the Holy Spirit transforms. My call is to cherish, not change.

I also don't believe Rafael is my *better half*,
and I am certainly not his. We are not two broken pieces trying to make a whole; we are two whole people, complete in Christ,
walking together toward Him.

Rafael is not the missing part of me,
he is my perfect complement. Where I am soft, he is steady.
Where I am expressive, he is measured. Where I see the world in words, he sees it in action. Together, we mirror a fullness that already exists in God.

So I made a decision early in our marriage: to love him in all his beautiful messiness; to hold space for the ways God is still forming him, and to let his process be as sacred as my own.

Rafael's love is deliberate. It's quiet, consistent, and tangible.
Before he came, no one asked what I had eaten, or if I'd made it home safely, or if the weight I carried that day was too much to bear alone.

But Rafael's love showed up; in dinners cooked,
in questions asked, in presence that did not leave.

It was steady, thoughtful, intentional; a love that is verb first, feeling later. Almost a decade later, I rest from the noise of life
knowing he keeps his vows not by sentiment but by practice.
He loves with his hands, with his patience, with his yeses.

Our marriage is a threefold cord—not easily broken, because God is the thread between us.

Guardrails of Grace

Boundaries are not punishment. They are protection.

There was a time when I misunderstood boundaries.
I thought they were a response to failure… something you put in place
after something breaks.
Or worse, I thought they were a form of control… a quiet way of
saying, *"I don't trust you."*

But healing taught me something different.

Boundaries are not built from fear. They are built from honor.

They are the guardrails that protect what God has called sacred.
Not walls that keep love out,
but wisdom that keeps love from being handled carelessly.

In a covenant, you don't wait for destruction to build protection.
You guard what is valuable because it already is.

For us, boundaries became a language… a quiet, consistent way of
saying: **"This matters to me. Us matters to me."**

That meant choosing transparency, even in places where it would be
easier to be private. Not because we live under suspicion, but because
we refuse to give secrecy a place to grow. We learned that emotional
distance rarely begins with something dramatic.

It starts in small, hidden spaces,
conversations unshared,
connections unaccounted for,
moments that slowly drift outside of "us."

So we stay open.
Not perfect, but open.

It also meant protecting the intimacy that belongs inside our marriage.
Not just physical intimacy, but emotional and spiritual closeness.
There are conversations, vulnerabilities, and depths of connection that
are not meant to be scattered across other relationships.

Not because other people are a threat,
but because not everything is meant to be shared with everyone.

There are parts of me that belong to my covenant.
And I guard them accordingly.

We also learned that love cannot survive on leftover time.
So we choose each other on purpose.
In the middle of schedules, responsibilities, children, ministry, and life's constant demands,
we come back to one another intentionally.

Because connection is not automatic. It is cultivated.

And sometimes, boundaries look like saying no.
No to environments that blur lines.
No to situations that seem harmless but carry unnecessary risk.
No to anything that would require us to explain away discomfort later.

Not out of fear, but out of reverence.

Because we have learned this truth:
Most betrayals do not begin with a decision.
They begin with a drift.

And boundaries are how we interrupt the drift before it becomes damage.

Boundaries are not restrictive. They are protective.

They keep love soft. They keep trust intact. They keep the covenant covered.

They say, without needing to be spoken out loud:
"I will not treat what we have casually."

And in a world that treats commitment like something temporary,
that kind of intentional guarding is not weakness…

It is worship.

When Trust Breaks

Betrayal shatters what feels unshakable.
It strikes at the soul of marriage… trust. And yet, even here, God
specializes in redemption.

Healing begins with honesty: acknowledging the pain,
inviting God into the fracture, and letting grace rebuild what pride once
protected.

Betrayal: whether in lies, neglect, or disappointment—
does not have to define the story.
Grace can rewrite it.

Forgiveness is not pretending the wound didn't happen.
It's choosing to let God touch the place you cannot fix.
It's releasing bitterness before it calcifies into distance.

Grace looks your spouse in the eye and says:
"I still see you. Not because you are perfect, but because God is still
working in you."

Catching the Little Foxes

Scripture warns us:
"Catch for us the foxes, the little foxes that ruin the vineyards."

-Song of Solomon 2:15

In marriage, those foxes are rarely dramatic.
They are small annoyances, half-finished conversations, unspoken
expectations. If left unattended, they nibble at the roots of trust.

I remember early in our marriage,
Rafael's love showed up in the most practical ways:
grocery lists, bedtime routines,
shoveling snow before I woke up.
He delighted in the daily details that once overwhelmed me.

But part of me, still healing from my past, misread his attentiveness as
control.

I carried an old script that whispered, *"If he's involved, he must not trust you."*

Then one day, he told me quietly, "I waited my whole life for this... to be a husband, a father, a provider. I don't want to miss a single moment of what God gave me."

That moment changed me. What I thought was criticism was care. What felt like intrusion was devotion. And what I had labeled controlling was actually **love expressed through responsibility.**

Sometimes healing requires re-seeing what love has always been trying to say. Now, when I notice those small irritations rise,
I stop and remember:
he loves differently, but he loves fully.

Grace and the Daily Washing

Forgiveness is the laver of marriage.

Just as the priests once washed before entering the holy place,
we must wash our hearts in prayer
before we speak, before we respond, before we keep score.

Every act of grace cleanses the residue of pride.
Every apology opens the door for intimacy to return.
Every "I forgive you" whispers to heaven,
"We still believe in covenant love."

I think about Peter.

After his betrayal, Jesus did not shame him. He restored him.

Three affirmations of love for three denials. Not to erase what happened, but to redeem it.

That is the way of grace. It does not ignore failure. It transforms it.

And in marriage, it does the same. What once broke you can become the very place God binds you stronger than before.

When Grace Becomes a Lifestyle

Grace is not reserved for the moments that nearly destroy you.
It lives in the small, daily places.

The sigh before an apology. The pause before a harsh word.
The decision not to rehearse an old offense.

It meets us in the ordinary frictions of marriage: the missed call, the tired silence, the unspoken disappointment. Because not all betrayal roars. Sometimes, it whispers. Through neglect. Through tone. Through distance that goes unaddressed.

But when grace becomes your rhythm, those moments no longer divide you. They invite you.

To soften. To re-see. To choose love again.

Grace does not excuse what hurts. It looks at the wound and says, **"This, too, can be healed."**

It chooses connection while trusting God to finish the work He began in both hearts.

Marriage will stretch you. It will expose what is unhealed and refine what is real. But covenant love is not sustained by perfection. It is sustained by grace.

By the daily decision to stay, to soften, to forgive, and to begin again.

The Forgiveness Journal

A Daily Practice of Grace

Forgiveness is not a one-time event, it's a daily posture.
It's the quiet work of releasing what you cannot carry
and inviting God to fill the space bitterness once occupied.

These journal pages are a sacred space to process, release, and rebuild.
It's where you confront the small foxes that threaten your peace
and make room for grace to take root again.

Use this space to reflect on what forgiveness looks like
in your heart, your marriage, and your walk with God.

Date:
What I Need to Release Today:
Write honestly about the offense, fear, or memory that lingers.
(Example: "The resentment I feel when I'm misunderstood.")

_____

_____

_____

_____

What I'm Choosing Instead:
Identify what you'll exchange it for—peace, compassion, hope.
(Example: "I choose to believe God can restore understanding between us.")

_____

_____

_____

_____

Scripture Connection:

Find a verse that speaks to forgiveness or grace.

(Example: "Ephesians 4:32 — Be kind and compassionate to one another, forgiving each other, just as in Christ God forgave you.")

_____

_____

_____

_____

Prayer of Surrender:

Write a short prayer offering the situation to God.

(Example: "Lord, teach me to forgive as You forgive. Heal what I cannot fix and restore what I have released to You.")

_____

_____

_____

_____

Act of Renewal:

Describe one tangible way you'll walk out this forgiveness today.

(Example: "I will speak with kindness even when I still feel hurt.")

_____

_____

_____

_____

The Spiritual Truth

- Fidelity is the daily choosing of faithfulness in heart, mind, and body.

- Forgiveness is mercy in motion—an act of worship that keeps love soft.

- Boundaries protect what God has joined; grace restores what we've wounded.

- Trust is not rebuilt overnight; it's rebuilt through honesty, humility, and time.

"Above all, love each other deeply, because love covers a multitude of sins."

— *1 Peter 4:8*

Reflection Pause

Where have I confused control with care?

_____

_____

_____

What small "foxes" are nibbling at the edges of our peace?

_____

_____

_____

_____

How is God asking me to guard what He's already healed?

_____

_____

_____

_____

What boundary would make our love feel safer—not stricter, but stronger?

_____

_____

_____

_____

Simple Breath Prayer

Lord, teach us to be faithful in thought as well as deed.
Keep our words gentle and our hearts clean.
Catch the little foxes before they grow into distance.
Wash our love daily in grace until it shines again.
Amen.

My prayer for you…

May loyalty be your language,
grace your guardrail,
and forgiveness the daily washing
that keeps your love holy.

_____

_____

_____

_____

_____

_____

_____

_____

_____

_____

_____

Selah

Pause here.
Let your heart take a breath.

"Grace is not the absence of pain;
it is the presence of God in the middle of it."

Chapter 3

Balancing Ministry with Marriage

When Calling Consumes Covenant

"Come with Me by yourselves to a quiet place and get some rest."

— Mark 6:31

Before I understood balance, I misunderstood obedience.

I thought saying yes to God meant saying yes to everything.
Every prayer request, I carried.
Every event, I attended.
Every emergency, I absorbed.
Every burden, I picked up, even when it was never mine to hold.

I fasted for everyone and their mama, even when they were unwilling to fast for themselves. I poured out until there was nothing left to pour and called it holy.

Work. Church. Home. That was the rhythm.
No rest. No laughter. No stillness.

I thought exhaustion was evidence of devotion. I thought busyness proved my anointing. I thought depletion was just the cost of being called.

I was always at church. Lights on. Doors open. Planning. Leading. Cleaning. Praying for others while quietly falling apart myself.

I wore service like armor and called it surrender.

But somewhere along the way, I stopped hearing God in the silence.

The truth is, I did not know how to sit with Him in silence. I only knew how to serve Him. I could discern for others, but not for myself. I could recognize His presence in the sanctuary, but not in Jelani's basketball games, not in time laughing with Jelise, not in the simple quiet of being with Rafael when nothing needed to be produced.

I began to confuse His presence with my performance.

I thought being busy for God meant being close to God, but what I had really built was an altar of exhaustion.

One day, sitting in my car after another long service, I felt the Holy Spirit whisper, not with rebuke, but with mercy:

Daughter, I never asked you to die on the altar I already filled.

That whisper broke me open.

It was the moment I realized I had confused ministry for God with intimacy with God. I was serving His people, but starving His presence. I was available to everyone, but unavailable to my own soul.

And if I am honest, there were times when I was unavailable to my husband too.

It was time to learn a new rhythm. One where calling did not consume covenant. One where my yes to ministry no longer came at the expense of my marriage, my children, my body, or my peace.

Marriage as Your First Ministry

It is impossible to be a blessing to everyone else while being a wound to the person you vowed to love.

That may sound strong, but I mean it.

Ministry begins at home. If your marriage is constantly absorbing the impact of your service, if your spouse only gets what is left of you after everyone else has taken their portion, then **something is out of order.**

I speak from experience.

Before Rafael and I married, I had already been ordained as a pastor for five years. By then, ministry was not just something I did. It was woven into my identity. Worship. Youth leadership. Intercession. Dance. Service. Presence. Availability. For fifteen years before meeting Rafael, the church world had my focus, my energy, and in many ways, my sense of self.

So, when I got married, I thought I understood what covenant would require.

I did not.

I knew how to serve the church. I did not yet know how to serve a home.

Early in our marriage, I was still juggling countless ministry commitments while trying to learn how to be a wife. Rafael never asked me to abandon ministry. He was not trying to compete with God, and he was certainly not threatened by my calling. What he wanted was partnership. Presence. Connection. A life that felt shared, not scheduled around me.

And in his gentle, consistent way, he became a mirror.

He showed me that while I had learned how to show up publicly, I was still learning how to be fully present privately.

He is a pastor too, but Rafael is an intercessor who prefers to preach in practice. His ministry is quiet. Steady. Tangible. He models Christ in the small faithful things: fixing every broken thing, checking in, grounding the atmosphere when I am moving in ten directions at once. His life says what many sermons never reach.

Where I am expressive, he is measured.
Where I am fiery, he is steady.
Where I can sometimes overextend, he anchors.

And somewhere in the middle of learning him, I had to learn that his needs were not interruptions to my calling.

They were part of it.

There were seasons when Rafael needed more of me than I knew how to give at first. Not because he was demanding, but because marriage is living, breathing, and holy. It asks for presence. It asks for attention. It asks for tenderness. It asks you to notice when your spouse is carrying too much and not assume covenant can survive indefinitely on good intentions.

I had prayed for a husband for seven years before Rafael arrived. How could I ask God for such a gift and then refuse to tend it?

That realization shifted something in me.

I began to understand that honoring my husband was not choosing him over God. It was one of the ways I honored God.

Marriage is not a side assignment. It is not what you manage after you finish doing "real ministry." It is one of the clearest reflections of Christ's covenant love many people will ever see.

And if I neglected that reflection, what exactly was I preaching?

A Sacred Reckoning

When we found out we were pregnant with Jeliel, it felt like God had breathed fresh life into our home.

After years of pouring into others, this was joy of another kind. Promise. Tenderness. A new stretching. A sacred weight we welcomed with love.

But even in that holy season, I slipped back into my old rhythm.

Doing. Pushing. Carrying more than I was ever meant to carry.

I told myself I could keep up the same pace. I told myself ministry did not need to slow down just because my body was changing. I thought I could muscle through sacred transition the same way I had survived other seasons.

I was wrong.

The exhaustion caught up with me quickly. I was sick. The reflux was relentless. The stress was constant. My body was signaling distress, but I kept trying to medicate symptoms instead of listening to what my body, and honestly what God, were trying to say.

What started as discomfort turned into weeks of real weakness. Forty-five days. Weight loss. Fatigue. Diminishing strength. I was trying to keep functioning while something in me was clearly failing.

And again, Rafael became my mirror.

He prayed over me. Cooked for me. Stayed near me when I could barely eat. He was gentle, never condemning, but his presence exposed what I had tried to avoid: this was not just physical fatigue. This was spiritual misalignment.

It was a reckoning.

We made a vow before the Lord. A costly one. One that required surrender not just spiritually, but financially and emotionally too. We chose to reorder our lives around obedience instead of obligation.

I stepped away from work.
I stepped away from serving for a season.
I got quiet enough to hear what I had been outrunning.

And in that quiet, God began healing more than my body.

He healed the rhythm of our marriage.
He healed my understanding of service.
He healed the lie that faithfulness and over functioning were the same thing.

He reminded me that calling should never consume covenant.

He showed me that honoring Rafael and nurturing what God had placed inside me were both acts of worship.

That season stripped me of ministry titles, deadlines, expectations, and the endless need to prove my usefulness. Until, in many ways, only three identities remained before God:

Wife. Mother. Daughter.

And in that posture, I finally understood that obedience sometimes looks like rest. Holiness sometimes looks like saying no. Love sometimes looks like staying home. And the same God who called me to serve was also calling me to be still.

Unlearning the Myths of Ministry and Marriage

This part required unlearning.

For years, I had absorbed religious narratives that sounded spiritual but were actually harmful. The idea that real devotion meant self-erasure. The idea that saying yes to God meant saying no to your own limits. The idea that being constantly available was some kind of proof of purity. The idea that if your marriage struggled under the weight of ministry, that was just part of the cost.

No.

That was never God's design.

We have made idols out of exhaustion in some church spaces. We celebrate the couple that is everywhere, doing everything, always needed, always moving, always visible. We admire the "power couple" image and often fail to ask whether they actually have peace at home, tenderness in private, or room to breathe.

The goal is not to look impressive in ministry.

The goal is to remain whole enough to love well.

Rafael taught me this in the way he lives. He never needed a stage to prove his spirituality. His quiet leadership is as sacred as my public expression. His consistency is as anointed as my fire. His steadiness is not lesser ministry. It is ministry with roots.

Together, we have had to dismantle myths about what a Godly marriage is supposed to look like. We have had to stop measuring ourselves against religious performance and make room for our own rhythm.

And that rhythm is not built on perfection. It is built on intention.

Balance is not something you find. It is something you cultivate. It is a returning. A reordering. A willingness to ask, again and again: What matters most right now, and what would faithfulness look like here?

The Boundaries That Brought Peace

At some point, Rafael and I had to stop assuming balance would happen naturally. It never does and probably never will.

We had to name our non-negotiables. Family dinners. No ministry travel during key family moments. Real Sabbath rest in the form of Saturday Adventures. Time together with no agenda. Time with the children that did not feel rushed or squeezed in. Space to laugh. Space to be quiet. Space to just be married, not useful.

And to my surprise, creating those boundaries did not feel like loss.

It felt like peace.

I learned that saying no to some ministry opportunities was not rebellion. It was not selfishness. It was not spiritual laziness. Sometimes it was the deepest yes I could offer to God, because it was a yes rooted in order, covenant, and truth.

We cannot give our marriages whatever scraps remain after everyone else has eaten.

That is not sacrifice. That is negligence dressed up in church clothes.

A healthy marriage requires guarding. Not because love is fragile, but because it is sacred. And sacred things deserve protection.

A Few Practices That Helped Us

I do not believe balance comes from complicated systems. I think it comes from honest rhythms.

These are a few that helped us:

Communicate Honestly

We had to learn how to say what was true before resentment said it for us. Not every conversation needed to be dramatic. Sometimes it was as simple as, "I miss you." Or, "This week is too full." Or, "I need you with me, not just near me."

Honest communication built safety for us. Not polished communication. Not pastor language. Honest language.

James 1:19 — "Everyone should be quick to listen, slow to speak, and slow to become angry."
Active listening creates safety. When we slow down enough to hear, we build trust.

> **Practice:** Schedule short daily check-ins to share gratitude, frustrations, or prayer requests. Connection grows in consistent conversation.

Honor Your Differences

I had to stop expecting Rafael to love, lead, and serve exactly the way I do. He is not me in male form, thank God.

His strengths are different. His style is different. His rhythm is different. And those differences are not obstacles to unity. They are part of how God designed our covenant to work.

1 Corinthians 12:4–6 reminds us there are many gifts, but one Spirit. Rafael's quiet strength and my passionate drive are not contradictions—they're complements.

> **Practice:** Name your spouse's strengths aloud this week. Acknowledge the ways they reflect Christ differently than you do.

Set Boundaries Together

Boundaries stopped being theoretical when we realized ministry would take as much as we offered it.

So we got clear.
What is ours to carry? What belongs to this season? What can wait? What must be protected?

Boundaries are not punishment. They are stewardship.

Proverbs 4:23 — "Guard your heart, for everything you do flows from it."
Boundaries are holy. They preserve joy and keep ministry from becoming the third person in your marriage.

> **Practice:** Protect your non-negotiables. Let family time, prayer, and rest stand firm on your calendar.

Prioritize Rest

Rest is not a reward for collapse. It is a rhythm of trust.

I had to learn that the world would not fall apart if I sat down or took a nap. The church would survive if I missed a meeting. God did not need me to prove my devotion by running myself into the ground.

Rest is holy.

Genesis 2:2–3 shows us that even God rested.
Rest is not rebellion; it's reverence.

> **Practice:** Schedule rest intentionally. Use that time to laugh, to worship, or to simply be.

Seek Wise Counsel

There is wisdom in letting people who love God and love marriage speak into your life. Not everyone deserves a front-row seat to your covenant, but wise counsel can keep you from drifting into isolation, burnout, or pride.

You do not have to figure everything out alone.

Proverbs 11:14 teaches that victory comes through many counselors. Invite wisdom into your marriage. Healthy mentors help you see what love can look like in every season.

> **Practice:** Meet quarterly with a couple whose faith and relationship you admire. Let iron sharpen iron.

The Balance Journal

"Be still, and know that I am God." — *Psalm 46:10*

Balance is not something we stumble into. It is something we return to.

Somewhere beneath the noise, your soul already knows the difference between striving and obedience. Somewhere beneath the pressure, your body remembers what peace feels like. Somewhere beneath the endless demands, God is still inviting you to come away with Him.

Before the next assignment, the next sermon, the next meeting, the next yes, pause.

Remember that you, too, are someone God wants to tend.

He delights in your being, not just your doing.

Use this space to ask:

What am I carrying that was never assigned to me?

Where has my service become a hiding place?

What would it look like to love God without abandoning myself?

What does my spouse need from me that my schedule keeps postponing?

Where is God inviting me into a holier rhythm?

_____

_____

_____

_____

_____

_____

_____

Reflection Pause

1. What areas of my life feel out of rhythm right now, and what is God inviting me to release?

_____

_____

_____

2. How do I define obedience, and does that definition include rest?

_____

_____

_____

3. When was the last time I felt God's pleasure in my stillness rather than my service?

_____

_____

_____

4. What boundary or rhythm can I introduce this week that honors both my covenant and my calling?

_____

_____

_____

5. How does my marriage reflect God's character to those I serve?

Write freely. Let honesty flow without editing. This is not a test of holiness but an invitation to healing.

_____

_____

_____

Simple Breath Prayer

Inhale: *You are my peace, Lord.*
Exhale: *You are my pace.*

Inhale: *You order my steps.*
Exhale: *You quiet my striving.*

Inhale: *Teach me to serve with balance.*
Exhale: *Teach me to love from rest.*

Now close your eyes.
Breathe slowly, deeply, and picture the sacred spaces of your life —
your home, your marriage, your ministry — all resting under one
divine rhythm.
Ask the Holy Spirit to weave grace through every place where
exhaustion once lived.

When you're ready, whisper softly:

"Lord, let my first ministry always be the one that bears Your image in
my home."

My prayer for you…

May you learn to serve without striving, to love without depletion, and
to lead from the overflow of God's presence.
May your home be the first altar, your family the first congregation, and
your rest the most sacred offering.
May you remember that balance is not found in perfection, but in
presence.

_____

_____

_____

_____

_____

Selah

Pause here.
Let your soul find its rhythm again.

"Holiness is not in the hustle;
it's in the quiet where love learns to breathe."

Part Two-
Motherhood

Chapter 4

The Gift of Motherhood

When a Child Becomes the Turning Point

"Children are a heritage from the Lord, offspring a reward from Him."

— Psalm 127:3

Motherhood is often spoken about like a soft and glowing thing.

A blessing. A gift. A sacred calling.

And it is.

But sometimes the gift comes wrapped in fear.
Sometimes the calling arrives while you are still a child yourself.
Sometimes the blessing does not enter a peaceful life.
Sometimes it enters wreckage, and by the mercy of God, becomes the beginning of rescue.

That is what motherhood was for me.

It did not begin in stability.
It did not begin with a plan.
It did not begin in a safe home, a healthy marriage, or a life that looked ready to receive a child.

It began in chaos. In youth. In fear. In the kind of brokenness that makes your future feel already decided.

And yet, even there, God entrusted me with life.

The Day Everything Changed

I was eighteen years old when I saw two pink lines on a pregnancy test.

I was still a girl in so many ways. A junior in high school. Already carrying legal trouble, expulsion hearings, and the weight of a world that had taught me to expect dysfunction before peace. Domestic violence, gangs, juvenile delinquency, instability, trauma, these were not distant ideas to me. They were the landscape I was living in.

I had already been arrested three times. Serious charges hung over my future. The road ahead looked dark, and if I am honest, I was heading in that direction fast.

Then I found out I was pregnant. And everything changed.

Not all at once. Not magically. Not like the movies where one realization fixes everything.

But something in me shifted.

I knew I was carrying a boy. I had seen him in a dream three years earlier. God had let me see him before I was ready to understand why. He knew I would need to see it before I could believe it when the moment came.

That child, the one I would name Jelani Gabriel, became a turning point in my life long before he ever took his first breath.

I did not choose motherhood because I felt prepared.
I chose it because I knew this life mattered.
And in choosing him, I began, little by little, to choose life for myself too.

Jelani became the anchor God used to stop my drift.

He grounded me in an unwavering determination to become better, because I knew he would be watching. He would always be watching. And he was worth the fight.

Motherhood as a Divine Assignment

When I think about motherhood now, I do not think of it first as biology. I think of it as assignment.

Sacred assignment.
Divine stewardship.
A calling that asks everything from you and somehow still gives you more than it takes.

God chose me for my children.

Not because I was polished. Not because I was healed.
Not because I had all the tools I should have had.

He chose me in my immaturity. He chose me in my fear. He chose me in my becoming. And that truth has carried me through every season when I felt unequipped.

Jelani Gabriel is everything I never knew I always wanted.

From the moment I felt his tiny feet press against my ribs, my love for him was fierce. Protective. Unrelenting. I did not have a roadmap, but I had a resolve. I wanted to give him the life I never had. I wanted him to know stability I had never known, tenderness I had rarely seen, and faith I was only beginning to understand for myself.

Motherhood did not arrive when I was already strong.
It made strength necessary.

Motherhood did not ask me to be perfect.
It asked me to show up.

And that is what I kept trying to do.

There were many days I did not know what I was doing. Days when I felt swallowed by responsibility. Days when I was still growing up while raising someone who depended on me for everything. But even then, God's grace met me. Again and again. In exhaustion. In fear. In the not-enoughness of young motherhood.

Philippians 4:13 became more than a verse to me. It became survival language.

I can do all things through Christ who strengthens me.

Not because I felt strong.
But because I had no choice except to lean on the One who was.

The Trauma of His Birth

Motherhood changed my life before Jelani was born.
But his birth changed my body, my mind, and my spirit in ways I was not prepared for.

I did not know I had scoliosis. I did not know my spine would complicate labor. I did not know the epidural would fail because of the curvature in my back. I did not know how much pain a body could endure and remain conscious inside it.

I was induced. The contractions came hard and fast.

But my pelvic bone would not spread. It was called incompetent. With every contraction, my son's head pressed downward and his tiny heart could not tolerate the stress. His heart stopped.

My baby died inside of me.

I was rushed into an emergency C-section.

And I felt everything.

The epidural had not taken. The scalpel cut through my body, and I screamed louder than I ever had in my life, loud enough for Mami to hear me from the waiting room. They moved quickly. They got him out. I caught a glimpse of his tiny foot before they put me under from the pain.

When I woke up, I was alone in recovery.

My body was covered in ice packs to bring down the swelling and pain. I was terrified, disoriented, and too young to know how to process what had just happened. I did not know where my baby was. I did not know if he had survived. I honestly did not know if I had.

And though I could not name it then, I know now that this was the beginning of postpartum depression for me.

The Darkness That Followed

For three days, I could not hold Jelani.

My body felt foreign. My mind felt flooded. My spirit felt far away.

I loved my son, but trauma had built a wall between my love and my ability to feel joy inside it. For two years, I battled postpartum depression without language for it. I did not know what to call heaviness. I only knew I felt numb, ashamed, exhausted, and deeply afraid.

I thought I should have been stronger.
I thought I should have been more capable.
I thought something was wrong with me because motherhood had arrived with so much darkness attached to it.

84

But even there, God did not leave me.

And neither did my son.

Jelani became light in a season I could barely see through. His laughter cut through despair. His tiny hands holding mine reminded me that I was still here, still capable of love, still chosen to mother this child even when I felt broken by the responsibility of it.

He saved me in every way a person can be saved.

I have told him this many times, and I mean it every time.

He pulled me out of a life that was spiraling. He gave me a reason to fight for a different future. He gave me someone to become for.

And in many ways, we grew up together.

He saw the worst of me.
The unhealed parts.
The traumatized parts.
The parts still trying to separate survival from identity.

And still, he loved me.

The Children who Came After

Motherhood did not get easier simply because I had already entered it.

Between Jelani and Jelise, I lost a baby at five months pregnant.

That loss did not happen in a vacuum. My body was already carrying damage I did not fully understand at the time. Years of unknown and untreated infections from marital infidelity had left its mark on the inside - scar tissue in my fallopian tubes and damage in my reproductive system that would affect me for years to come. What I could not name then, I understand now: my body had been through more than I realized, and it was carrying the evidence of pain long after the moments themselves had passed.

There are griefs that never fully become language.
They live in the body. In the memory. In the way you flinch when joy
feels too vulnerable to trust.

That loss was one of them.

And if I am honest, there was another layer to that grief I did not know
how to admit at the time.

I was scared.

I loved Jelani so deeply, so fiercely, that I did not know if my heart had
room for another child. I did not know if love could multiply like that. I
did not know if I could divide myself again and still give him
everything he deserved.

But losing that baby taught me something I could not have learned any
other way.

My heart did not have a limit.
It had depth I had not yet discovered.

That loss revealed that love does not divide.
It expands.

And even in grief, God was stretching my capacity to become a mother
again… differently.

By the time I became pregnant with Jelise, my life was unraveling. I was
in a deeply abusive marriage, carrying life in the middle of collapse.

If I am honest, there was a moment I considered not continuing the
pregnancy.

That is hard to say out loud. But it is the truth.

Not because I did not value life, but because I did not know how I was
going to sustain it. I was already overwhelmed. Already stretched.
Already trying to survive. And now I was facing the reality of doing it
alone.

But somewhere in that breaking, I made a decision.

I would have her.
Not out of pressure. Not out of fear. But as a vow.

A vow to God. A vow to myself.
A vow that this life would not be another casualty of the chaos I was living in. I chose to bring her into the world and raise her, even if I had to do it alone.

And I did. What makes her story even more tender is this:

After my miscarriage, I spent two years trying to have another baby. Trying. Hoping. Obsessing. Praying. Waiting. And nothing came. It was only when I finally let go, when I released the grip I had on what I thought motherhood needed to look like next, that she came.

Unexpected. Unannounced. Unplanned in the way I thought I needed.

I never saw her coming.

I had dreams before. I saw two boys; one about four years old, and another in a baby seat. I believe I saw the son I lost. God let me see him.

But I never dreamed of Jelise.

I thought she was a boy for the longest time. I kept receipts for everything I bought, just in case I needed to take it all back. Because I did not know how to prepare for what I had never seen.

But when she came, she did something I did not expect.

She made space in my heart. Not by forcing it open,
but by letting light in slowly.

Jelise taught me that healing does not always come like a door flung wide open. Sometimes it comes like sunlight through a window. Quiet. Gentle. Persistent. She did not just enter my life.
She softened it.

Her birth, however, came with its own trauma.

My body was still carrying the physical consequences of years of brokenness. My uterus would not stop bleeding after delivery. It took six doses of medication to get the bleeding under control. The surgeon wanted to remove my uterus completely to stop it. They were that concerned. In many ways, I came dangerously close to losing my life. And by God's mercy, another path worked. But the aftermath did not end there.

Postpartum depression came again. This time it lasted nearly a year. I lived in a fog of sadness and fear, trying to cling to the joy my daughter brought while drowning in the dysfunction surrounding us.

I loved her fiercely, but love did not erase the weight I was carrying. It only made me more desperate to survive it. So, when I made the decision to have tubal ligation at twenty-four, it was not casual. It was not disconnected from grief. It was not a neat, empowered decision made from a place of abundance.

It was survival.

It was me looking at the two children I already had and deciding that they deserved to keep their mother. Like so many decisions women make in pain, it was not made in full freedom, but in the hope of preventing more suffering. At the time, it felt like the closing of a door.

And not just any door. I had always dreamed of having three children. That dream lived quietly inside me, even through the chaos, even through the trauma, even when life did not look anything like what I had imagined.

But in that moment, I let it go. Like I had let go of so many other things.

Dreams of ease.
Dreams of stability.
Dreams of becoming who I once thought I would be.

Even the dream of being an author felt distant back then. Life had a way of reshaping everything I thought I knew. And motherhood, as beautiful as it was, often felt like something I was surviving more than something I was getting to fully experience.

So, I closed that door. Bolted it shut.

Not because I stopped desiring it, but because I did not believe it was available to me anymore.

Some dreams don't die. They wait for the version of you that can finally receive them. And in time, God will bring you to that version.

The Miracle I Did Not Expect

And yet God, in His mercy, is still a God of astonishment.

Years later, in a new marriage with Rafael, He made a way for Jeliel through IVF.

And I did not experience that as medicine alone. I experienced it as mercy.

He was a miracle, yes, but more than that, he was a second chance.

Not a second chance to love, because I loved all my children fiercely from the beginning.

But a second chance to experience motherhood differently.
More fully. More consciously. More healed.

With Jelani and Jelise, so much of motherhood was survival.

I was working. Grinding. Struggling.
Mothering under pressure.
Missing pivotal moments because poverty, trauma, and spiritual overextension kept demanding more than I had to give.

I was often trying to keep everyone alive; emotionally, spiritually, materially and I did not always know how to simply enjoy them.

That grief is real too.

I cannot get those years back.
I cannot relive those early moments with softer hands, a calmer nervous system, or a life less burdened by lack. But I can show them something different now. With every breath I have left I can do the work.

And with Jeliel, God gave me a glimpse of redemption.

He let me taste motherhood with more presence.
More support. More wonder. More wholeness.

And though the shadow of postpartum depression returned, it did not devour me the same way. This time, I was not alone. Rafael stayed near me. He prayed with me. He encouraged me to seek help. I had language now. I had support. I had space to heal.

Jeliel's life became another testimony.

A reminder that God is able to bring beauty after devastation.
A reminder that what feels permanently closed in one season is not beyond resurrection in another.
A reminder that pain does not get the final word.

And that, too, was holy.

Motherhood Did Not Make Me Perfect

Motherhood transformed me.
But not neatly.

It stretched me. It exposed me. It confronted me.
It forced me to see the parts of myself that still needed healing.

I have made mistakes as a mother.

I have failed in moments when I wish I had been softer, steadier, slower to react, quicker to listen. There are moments I wish I could gather back into my hands and redo with more wisdom, more healing, more peace.

I cannot.

But I can tell the truth.

And the truth is this: God's grace has covered me in every season of motherhood, not because I mothered flawlessly, but because He knew I would need mercy as much as my children needed me.

I am not the mother my children needed because I was perfect.

I am the mother they were given because God knew what He was doing, even in my becoming.

That truth humbles me.

And it frees me.

Because motherhood is not about getting every moment right. It is about remaining willing to grow, willing to repair, willing to apologize, willing to keep becoming someone safer, wiser, and softer than the woman who began.

What My Children Taught Me

My children did not just receive my love.
They shaped it.

Jelani taught me that motherhood can interrupt destruction and turn it into destiny.
Jelise taught me that beauty can still bloom in seasons of deep pain.
Jeliel taught me that God still works miracles after final-seeming endings.

All three have taught me that motherhood is both altar and inheritance.

It is where you lay down selfishness, pride, illusions of control, and sometimes even old versions of yourself.

It is also where you receive tenderness, endurance, holy perspective, and the kind of love that keeps expanding your capacity.

Motherhood has been one of God's sharpest tools in my life.

Not because it always felt beautiful.
But because it kept making me tell the truth.

A Letter to My Son

When Jelani was young, I wrote him a letter. And even now, it still carries the truth of what I feel.

My Jelani Gabriel, strong man of God. The first time I met you, you were two pink lines on a pregnancy test. I had no clue who you would be, but even more than that, I had no clue who I would become once you entered my life. You saved me, son. You taught me how to love, how to hope, and how to trust God's plan.

You are my prodigy, my magnum opus. Through every mistake, every tear, and every triumph, you have been my anchor. I love every part of who you are, your strength, your gentleness, your wisdom beyond your years.

I am sorry for the moments when my unhealed trauma hurt you. Teen motherhood is hard, and I did not always get it right. But I promise to give you, your sister, and your little brother the best, healed version of myself moving forward. You are my warrior prince, my sonshine, and my greatest blessing. Never forget how deeply you are loved. Always be true to yourself, trust in God, and know that my love for you is fierce, unchanging, and unconditional.

There are some children you raise, and there are some children who, in the mystery of God, also raise you.

Jelani was that for me.

The Sacred Truth

Motherhood is a gift.

Not because it is easy. Not because every moment is glowing. Not because it comes without grief.

It is a gift because God entrusts us with souls.

He gives us the holy work of shaping, loving, guiding, correcting, covering, and praying over lives that do not belong to us, but pass through us.

Children are not interruptions to purpose.
They are purpose.

Motherhood is not a lesser calling.
It is one of the clearest reflections of the nurturing heart of God.

And if you have ever felt weak in it, unprepared for it, or broken by it, you are not disqualified.

You are human. And grace lives here too.

Finding Joy in Chaos

Motherhood is messy.

There are toys on the floor.
Questions with no end.
Sticky hands.
Interrupted thoughts.
Unfinished tasks.
Noise when you want quiet.
Silence when you want reassurance.

And yet, inside that chaos, there are holy moments.

A spontaneous hug. A laugh at the wrong time.
A sleepy face leaning into your shoulder. A tiny voice saying something profound without knowing it. A shared look that says, without words, *you are my safe place.*

The mess is not proof that you are failing. Sometimes it is proof that life is happening. I have learned that if I do not slow down, I will miss the beauty buried inside the inconvenience. And I do not want to spend my life cleaning up moments I never fully entered.

So, I have had to practice gratitude on purpose.

Not toxic gratitude. Not fake positivity. Real gratitude.

The kind that says:
This is hard. And this is holy.
This is loud. And this is love.
This is stretching me. And this is still a gift.

The Motherhood Journal

At the end of the day, pause and ask:

Where did I see grace in motherhood today?

What moment felt hard, but holy?

What did my child need from me today, and how did I respond?

Where do I need to forgive myself?

What small moment of joy do I want to remember before this season passes?

You do not need paragraphs.
You do not need polished insight.
You only need honesty.

One sentence of gratitude can become a lifeline in a weary season.

You might even begin a joy jar, a place to collect the moments you do not want motherhood's exhaustion to steal from your memory.

Because one day, what feels chaotic now may become the very thing you ache to hold again.

_____

_____

_____

_____

_____

_____

_____

_____

_____

Reflection Pause

How has God carried you through the hardest parts of motherhood?

_____

_____

_____

What have your children taught you about resilience, surrender, or love?

_____

_____

_____

Where have you judged yourself by a standard God never gave you?

_____

_____

_____

What part of your motherhood story still needs gentleness?

_____

_____

_____

How does seeing motherhood as a divine assignment change the way you hold today's challenges?

_____

_____

_____

Write honestly. Let the page hold what you have not always had words for.

_____

_____

_____

Simple Breath Prayer

Inhale: Lord, thank You for entrusting them to me.
Exhale: Help me mother with grace.

Inhale: Strengthen what feels weary.
Exhale: Soften what feels hardened.

Inhale: Teach me to see the holy in the ordinary.
Exhale: Remind me that I am not alone.

My Prayer for You

May you know that your motherhood matters, even on the days it feels invisible.

May God meet you in the sleeplessness, the mess, the fear, the laughter, the grief, and the ordinary miracles hidden inside your home.

May you remember that you do not have to mother perfectly to mother powerfully.

May grace cover every place where guilt once lived.

And may the same God who entrusted those children to you keep strengthening you to love them well.

_____

_____

_____

_____

_____

_____

_____

_____

Selah

Pause here.
Let your heart remember what your hands carry every day.

Motherhood is not small work.
It is soul work.
Holy work.
Kingdom work.

And somehow, in the giving of yourself, God gives you back to yourself too.

Chapter 5

Mothering in Faith
Walking in Grace While Raising What Belongs to God

"Train up a child in the way he should go; even when he is old he will not depart from it."
— Proverbs 22:6

I did not grow up imagining motherhood as my calling.

If I am honest, I never saw myself as the nurturing type. Motherhood felt like something that belonged to other women. Softer women. Women who knew how to braid hair without pulling too hard, who kept snacks in their purses, who instinctively knew what a child needed and when. That was never how I saw myself.

Truth be told, I still say it plainly: I do not really like kids.

Except mine. Mine are different. Mine are soul work.

Mine are the children God used to turn me inside out, to stretch my capacity for love, to confront the hardest parts of me, and to teach me how to walk with Him in a way that was not theoretical, but daily, costly, and real.

Motherhood did not come naturally to me.

Faith did not always either.

But grace met me in both.

Mothering Without a Map

I did not have a perfect model to follow.

Mami passed away when I was only twenty-one years old. Cancer took her before I could ask the questions daughters ask when they are standing on the edge of womanhood, marriage, motherhood, grief, and responsibility. She was not perfect, but she was mine. And there were questions I thought I would have time to ask later.

How did you do this?
How did you know when to be soft and when to be strong?
How did you hold children and yourself at the same time?
How did you keep going when life did not feel kind?

She was gone before I could ask. And that absence shaped me.

There is a particular ache in mothering while motherless. A quiet kind of disorientation. A missing reference point. A grief that shows up not only in funerals and anniversaries, but in school forms, fevers, daughters' questions, teenage sons, and every sacred moment where you realize you are becoming something you never got to fully witness up close.

I did not have a roadmap. But God, in His mercy, did not leave me without witness.

He surrounded me with women, with the Tribe. And thank God for the village.

Strategic women. Strong women. Tender women. Mothers, mentors, spiritual leaders, and elders who carried pieces of what I needed. No one woman gave me the whole picture, but together they formed a mosaic of wisdom, faith, correction, nurture, and strength.

I learned motherhood in fragments.

A little from one woman's gentleness.
A little from another's discipline.
A little from another's prayer life.
A little from another's way of listening.
A little from women who mothered me in spirit when life had already made me older than I should have been.

God taught me through many hands.

And looking back, that, too, was grace.

The Promise at the Altar

There are moments in your life that divide everything into before and after.

For me, one of those moments happened at an altar.

My first marriage had ended, and I was shattered. Not neatly hurt. Not quietly disappointed. Shattered.

I was raising Jelani and Jelise, carrying the weight of failure, shame, fear, and uncertainty like it was stitched into my skin. The burden of single motherhood felt unbearable. I was tired in every way a person can be tired. Emotionally. Financially. Spiritually. Physically.

And one day at church, all of it came crashing down.

I found myself face-down at the altar, weeping in the kind of way that does not care who is watching. I was not praying pretty. I was not holding myself together. I was undone. I begged God to take me because I could not see a way forward. I did not know how I was supposed to raise these children while carrying so much of my own brokenness.

And there, in that place of total collapse, the Lord met me.

Audibly and unmistakably.

He told me that if I would focus on His kingdom, He would help me raise my children.

That promise became my anchor.

Not because life got easy after that.
It did not.

Not because I suddenly became confident.
I also did not.

But because I knew I was no longer doing it alone.

That promise held me on days when I felt too weak to mother well. It held me when bills were high and patience was low. It held me when I felt guilty, uncertain, or ashamed. It held me when I could not see fruit yet. It held me when I was pouring into children while still healing the child in me.

God did not promise I would do it perfectly.

He promised He would help me. And He has.

Motherhood Through Grace, Not Perfection

My journey as a mother has not been polished.

It has been marked by grace.

Not the cheap kind. Not the kind that excuses everything and transforms nothing. I mean the kind of grace that holds you accountable while still holding you close. The kind that lets you tell the truth and keep going. The kind that does not deny the mistakes and refuses to let them become your final identity.

I have walked this road hand in hand with God.

Through joyful milestones and deep heartbreak.
Through triumph and terror.
Through whispered bedtime prayers and hard conversations.
Through school drop-offs and hospital visits.
Through discipline, laughter, conflict, repair, and all the holy monotony of showing up again tomorrow.

He has been my wisdom when I did not know what to do.
My patience when mine was gone.
My strength when motherhood pulled on every exposed wire in me.
My comfort when guilt was louder than grace.

And over time, I began to see something I had not understood at first:

My children were not interruptions to my life with God. They were one of the deepest places I would meet Him.

My Children as Love Songs

I have come to see my children as love songs I have written to the Lord.

Not because I made them perfectly.
Not because I have mothered flawlessly.
But because loving them has become one of the clearest ways I worship.

They are my most precious offerings.

They belonged to Him before they belonged to me.

That sentence was such a hard truth to swallow. That truth humbles me every time I really sit with it. These lives that call me Momma, the oones who know what my heart sounds like on the inside, my children. The ones I have kissed, corrected, prayed over, and fought for, they are entrusted to me, but they are not mine to possess. They are His.

And what an honor. What a weight. What a sacred thing.

I get to nurture what belongs to God. I get to speak over lives Heaven had in mind before I ever held them.

I get to stand in the gap between who they are now and who they are becoming, asking the Lord to shape them, cover them, preserve them, and call them forward.

That is not small work. That is holy work.

The Power of a Name

Mami used to say that a name is the most influential word a person will ever hear. At the time, I did not fully understand that. But motherhood made me understand quickly.

A name is never just a label.

It is identity. It is hope.
It is prophecy. It is intention spoken out loud over and over again.

I took that seriously when I named my children.

Not because I thought a good name could guarantee an easy life.
But because I wanted their names to carry meaning. Weight. Prayer. Direction.

I wanted their names to speak before the world ever tried to define them.

Jelani Gabriel

Jelani means strong, mighty or great. Gabriel means man of God.

My firstborn son needed a name with strength in it.

And maybe, if I am honest, so did I.

Every time I said his name, I was speaking destiny over him. Strength. Calling. Weight. Purpose. He was the child who made me a mother and the son who made me fight for my life in a different way.

When I call him Jelani Gabriel, I am not just calling for his attention. I am reminding him who he is.

Mighty.
Chosen.
A strong man of God.

And the beautiful thing is that he has lived up to that strength in ways that still humble me.

Jelise Anaelle

Jelise, my lioness. My vow to the Lord

Her name carries such duality - fierceness and covenant. Unshakeable determination rolled into femininity. Fragile. Not like crystal or glass, more like a bomb... that you better handle with extreme care understanding fully its power.

She entered my life in a season of collapse and still brought light. She taught me that strength does not always roar. Sometimes it arrives tender. Sometimes it enters softly and still changes the atmosphere of everything.

Her name is courage and consecration to me. A daughter who carries both boldness and beauty. A girl with a lion's heart who knows what she wants and carries a spirit that knows how to turn the hard things toward God.

When I say her name, I hear strength wrapped in promise.

Jeliel Izrael

And then came Jeliel.

God, my God who perseveres.
My miracle after doors I thought had permanently closed.

His name speaks of preservation.
Of the God who keeps going, keeps working, keeps making a way
when human logic has already concluded there is none.

His life is a declaration that what God speaks still stands.

Every time I call his name, I hear endurance. Mercy.
Promise. The faithfulness of a God who does not run out of surprises.

Jeliel did not just enter our lives. He restored something in them.

He is the child who carries wonder.

The one who sees life with a kind of safety the rest of us had to fight to
find. The one who laughs freely, trusts deeply, and experiences the
world without the weight that shaped so much of my early
motherhood.

There is something sacred about watching a child grow in an
atmosphere that is not defined by survival.

It is healing.

Not just for him… but for me.

Because through him, God did something I did not expect. He did not
just give me another child. He gave me another chance to witness
childhood differently.

To slow down. To be present. To enjoy what I once had to endure.

Jeliel is being shaped to dream without limitations. And somehow, in
that process, he is teaching us how to do the same.

He reminds me that not every story has to begin in struggle to be
meaningful. That joy is not something we have to earn through pain.
That God is just as present in the laughter as He was in the breaking.

He is our reminder that restoration is not just about recovering what was lost.

Sometimes, it is about receiving something entirely new...
something softer, freer, and full of wonder.

And that, too, is holy.

Speaking Life on Purpose

Naming them was only the beginning.

I have learned that the words we repeatedly speak over our children matter deeply. Names carry power, yes, but so do the daily declarations spoken into their hearing. So do the ways we narrate them. So do the things we repeat when they fail, when they shine, when they are confused, when they are becoming.

I have tried, however imperfectly, to speak life over my children.

To call out not only what is visible, but what is possible.
To affirm not only behavior, but identity.
To speak Scripture over them. To remind them who they are when life tries to hand them lesser names.

There is a difference between merely raising children and intentionally blessing them.

I wanted to do more than feed them, clothe them, and get them where they needed to go.

I wanted to plant language in them that would outlive me.

Language that says:

You are chosen.
You are loved.
You are not your worst moment.
You are not what broke our family.
You are not what this world expects from you.
You are who God says you are.
And I will keep saying it until you can hear it for yourself.

Loving Them As They Are

One of the most sacred parts of motherhood has been learning to love my children as they are, not as I imagined them to be.

That sounds simple. It is not.

Every parent carries some unspoken dream. Some imagined version of who their child will become. Some quiet hope, some fear, some preference, some expectation.

And if you are not careful, you can start loving the projection more than the person.

I never wanted that. But I struggled here for a long time.

I have learned that my role is not to mold my children into extensions of myself. My role is to guide them toward the identity God has already placed inside them. To help them recognize it. To nurture it. To correct without crushing. To cover without controlling. To bless without possessing.

They are all so different.

Jelani carries wisdom and weight.
Jelise carries courage and fire.
Jeliel carries joy and perseverance.

And loving them well has meant learning their languages, honoring their individuality, and refusing to confuse my preferences with God's design.

They are my children.
But they are not my copies.

And that is part of the beauty.

A Mother's Offering

When I think about motherhood in its deepest sense, I think of offering.

Not performance.
Not management.
Not image.

Offering.

I think of Hannah, who prayed for a son and then returned him to the Lord in surrender. My story is different, but I understand the posture. To mother is to hold tightly and surrender constantly. To love fiercely while remembering these lives are passing through your hands, not into your ownership.

My children are my offering to God.

Not because they are perfect.
Not because I am.
But because every prayer I whisper over them, every correction given with trembling, every sacrifice made in silence, every act of protection, every attempt to love them in truth, all of it becomes worship when placed before the Lord.

The daily rhythms of motherhood are full of hidden offerings.

The lunch packed.
The hard conversation had.
The tears wiped.
The prayers whispered over sleeping faces.
The apologies made when I get it wrong.
The covering.
The carrying.
The releasing.

This is how I sing love songs to the Lord now.

Not always with melody. Sometimes with carpools.
Sometimes with discipline. Sometimes with folded clothes and quiet prayers. Sometimes with tears. Sometimes with laughter.

But always with devotion.

What Faithful Mothering Looks Like for Me

Mothering in faith has not meant always knowing what to do.

It has meant staying close to God while I do not know.

It has meant letting my children see that dependence on God is not weakness. It is wisdom.

It has meant praying when I want to control.
Listening when I want to lecture.
Repenting when I get it wrong.
Blessing when I feel afraid.
Trusting God to do what I cannot force.

I am not raising perfect children.

I am raising human beings.

And I am doing it as a human being who still needs grace too.

That is why faith matters so much in motherhood.

Because without it, I would mistake responsibility for control. I would try to manufacture outcomes only God can produce. I would confuse my role as mother with His role as God.

But faith helps me remember:

I plant.
I water.
I pray.
I model.
I repent.
I love.

And God gives the increase.

A Prayer Journal for Mothers

Consider keeping a motherhood prayer journal.

Not because every prayer will be answered quickly.
Not because every season will make sense while you are in it.
But because remembrance builds faith.

Write down:

- prayers for each child

- Scriptures you are standing on

- what God has spoken in hard seasons

- the ways He answers, sustains, redirects, or comforts

Let it become a witness.

A record of God's faithfulness to your family.
A place where fear turns into intercession.
A place where hope has somewhere to live on paper when it feels
fragile in your chest.

_____

_____

_____

_____

_____

_____

_____

_____

Speaking Life: A Gentle Practice

Take time to speak intentional words over your children.

You do not need a podium.
You do not need perfect language.
You do not need to sound impressive.

You only need intention.

Call them by name.
Bless what God has planted in them.
Affirm their worth.
Speak Scripture over their minds, their bodies, their gifts, their future.

Plant language that will still echo when they are old enough to need it on their own.

Because every child will hear many voices in this world.

Let yours be one that reminds them who they are.

Reflection Pause

Where has God met me in the places I felt least equipped to parent?

_____

_____

_____

What promise from God has anchored me in motherhood?

_____

_____

_____

Who are the women God has used to shape me when I did not have a full model of my own?

_____

_____

_____

What names, labels, or narratives have I spoken over my children that need to be replaced with life?

_____

_____

_____

How can I better love my children as they are, not as I expected them to be?

_____

_____

_____

Write slowly. Let the truth rise without forcing it.

_____

_____

_____

Simple Breath Prayer

Inhale: Lord, help me raise what belongs to You.
Exhale: Teach me to mother in faith.

Inhale: Let my words plant life.
Exhale: Let my love reflect Yours.

Inhale: Strengthen me where I feel unsure.
Exhale: Remind me that grace is here too.

My Prayer for You

May God strengthen you in the quiet, hidden work of mothering.

May He meet you in the places where you feel unequipped and remind you that calling does not begin with confidence. It begins with surrender.

May the words you speak over your children become seeds of identity, faith, healing, and courage.

May you know that even if you were not mothered perfectly, you are not doomed to repeat what was missing.

Grace can teach you.
God can mother you while you mother them.
And wisdom can come in pieces and still become something beautiful.

_____

_____

_____

_____

_____

_____

Selah

Pause here.
Let your heart rest in this truth:

You do not have to mother from mastery.
You can mother from grace.

Chapter 6

When Ministry Meets Motherhood

Serving Without Abandoning What Calls You Momma

"She watches over the affairs of her household and does not

eat the bread of idleness."

— Proverbs 31:27

There were seasons when I felt split straight down the middle.

At church, I was needed. At home, I was needed.

In ministry, there was always one more person to pray for, one more crisis to respond to, one more yes that felt holy in the moment.

And at home, there were lunches to pack, tears to tend, questions to answer, moments to catch, and children who did not need a powerful woman on a microphone nearly as much as they needed their mother to be fully present.

That tension is not theoretical to me.

I have lived it.

I have prayed for other people's children while worrying about my own. I have poured out spiritually in rooms full of people and then come home so depleted that the ones I loved most got what was left of me instead of the best of me. I have felt guilty at church because home needed me, and guilty at home because ministry was calling.

So I tried to become everything.

I would do more.
Push harder.
Sleep less.
Carry both.
Call it sacrifice.

But eventually, God had to interrupt that version of me.

Because being needed in many places does not mean I am assigned to bleed out in all of them.

The Lie I Believed

Somewhere along the way, I believed something that sounded spiritual but was not.

That a good mother never drops anything.
That a faithful woman never says no.

123

That if I was truly called, I would be able to carry everything placed in front of me.

But that is not faithfulness. That is pressure.

And pressure will make you confuse:

- calling with capacity
- availability with assignment
- performance with obedience

So I kept saying yes.

Yes to ministry. Yes to people. Yes to expectations.

And without realizing it, I started saying no to what mattered most.

Presence. Attention. Rest. My children.

Not out of neglect. But out of misalignment.

The Moment My Son Called Me Back

There are moments in motherhood where God uses your children to confront you in ways no one else can.

This was one of those moments.

And parts of this story are not mine to tell in full.
They belong to my son.

But what I can say is this:

There was a season where Jelani was in crisis.

And in the middle of it… he called me out.

Not with disrespect. But with truth. And his truth broke something in me. Because I had to face what I had not fully confronted: I had not mothered him the way he deserved.

I had pushed him too hard. Too much discipline.
Not enough compassion. Not enough understanding.

I needed help when I was raising him. And instead of always getting it, I leaned on him.

I expected strength from a boy who needed covering.
Maturity from a child who deserved childhood.

And in doing that, I took something from him.

I missed games.
I missed moments.
I missed opportunities to simply be his mother.

Because I was working.
Because I was surviving.
Because I was serving.
Because I was trying to build something while still broken.

And I told myself it was necessary. I told myself it was sacrifice.

But in that moment, God made something painfully clear: He needed a mother.

Not a warrior.
Not a minister.
Not a woman trying to hold the world together.

A mother.

The Truth That Broke Me Open

There is a particular kind of pain that comes when you realize:

You did your best… and your best still left wounds.

That realization does not come with defense. It comes with surrender.
Because I had to say this out loud:

Jelani got the broken version of me.
Jelise got the version of me on the way.
And Jeliel…
he is getting the healed version.

And there is grief in that.

And that grief does not come with shame.
It comes with awareness.
It comes with a commitment that what I did not know then,
I will not ignore now.

Because Jelani deserved the healed version too.

The Question That Changed Everything

And this is the question that confronted me at my core:

If I cannot get this right,
then who have I been praying to?

Who have I believed in?

How can I call myself prophetic if I do not trust God to heal me first
before calling me to help heal others?

Because if I am building ministry while my own house is hurting…
then I have to ask myself a harder question:
Who am I really serving?

Because that is not Kingdom. That is control disguised as calling.
That is ego dressed up as obedience. That is performance trying to pass
as anointing.

And God is not in that.

God is not in what we build
when we have abandoned what He asked us to steward first.

Missing God on the Way to God

We do not talk about this enough in the Church.

We know how to:

- build ministries
- carry mantles
- show up for people

- operate in gifting

But we do not always know how to:

go home and be present.

We will pray for children in the altar and ignore our own at the dinner table. We will cast out demons in public and avoid hard conversations in private.

We will call it sacrifice. But sometimes... *we are missing God on the way to God.*

And it is a lie.

Because there is nothing holy about:

- abandoning your first assignment
- neglecting your children to prove your devotion
- building something public while something private is breaking

God does not require your family as collateral for your calling. He entrusted them to you as part of it.

Letting Go of the Version I Created

In that same season, Jelani forced something else in me.

He forced me to let go. To let go of:

- the version of him I had created
- the expectations I held too tightly
- the control I thought was protection

He is not mine to control. He is a man God is forming. And loving him meant releasing him. Not abandoning him.

But allowing him to live his life
while I remained his mother—present, covering, available.

Control can look like love. But it is not the same thing.

Learning to Receive Help

I also had to face this:

I was never meant to do this alone.

Not motherhood. Not ministry. But I resisted help for a long time. Because I thought needing people meant I was weak. But that was not strength. That was survival that had not learned how to trust.

God sends people:

- to help carry
- to support
- to cover
- to stand in the gap

Receiving help did not make me less of a mother. It made me a wiser one.

Redemption Is Still Available

And even in all of this… God showed me something I will never forget:

It is not too late. Not too late to:

- apologize
- listen
- love differently
- show up intentionally
- rebuild what was strained

He did not end our story in what I got wrong. He allowed space for restoration. And in His mercy… He saved my son.

And He is still healing both of us.

Raising Children Who Can Question You

Something shifted in me after that season with Jelani.

Not just how I loved him... but how I understood authority.

Because what I saw in him—his courage to speak, to challenge, to tell the truth even when it was uncomfortable—was not rebellion.

It was formation. And if I am honest, that realization stretched me. Because as a mother, especially one who had to survive and lead early, I had learned to associate authority with control.

With structure. With direction. With being right. But God began to show me something deeper:

Authority in the Kingdom is not about control.
It is about creating space for truth.

It is about being secure enough in what you carry
that you are not threatened when truth comes from someone else—
even when that someone is your child.

Because of Jelani, something opened in our home.

Jelise saw it too.

She saw that she could ask questions.
That she could express herself.
That she did not have to shrink to honor me.

And I had to decide what kind of mother I was going to be in that space.

The kind who demands silence to maintain control...

Or the kind who welcomes dialogue
because she trusts what she has planted.

I Do Not Have to Be Right to Be Their Mother

There is a humility that motherhood will require of you
if you are willing to grow.

I had to learn to say:

"I don't have all the answers."
"I may not see this clearly."
"Help me understand you."

And that did not diminish my authority. It purified it. Because my role
is not to be their source of all truth.

My role is to:

- guide
- cover
- model
- and point them to the One who is truth

They Are Not Becoming Me

This was another breaking point for me.

My children are not called to become me.

Not in how they:

- worship
- speak
- express themselves
- process God
- or move through life

And if I am not careful, I can mistake **difference for dishonor**.

But it is not dishonor. It is identity. They do not need to mirror me to be
holy. They need to become who God created them to be.

Fully.
Safely.
Authentically.

My Faith Cannot Save Them

This truth required the deepest surrender.

My faith cannot save my children.

My prayers cover them. My example guides them. My love surrounds them. But at some point… they must encounter God for themselves.

Not my version of Him. Not my language. Not my expression.

Their own.

And that means I cannot control their process. I can only prepare the ground.

Building the Bridge

This is what I now believe my role is:

To build a bridge.

Not to drag them across it.
Not to force them into experiences they have not owned.

But to **build something strong enough, safe enough, and loving enough**
that when they are ready…

they can cross it freely.

A bridge built with:

- truth
- consistency
- presence
- repentance when needed
- and love that does not withdraw

A bridge that connects: the heart of the Father, and the covering of a mother. So that when they step into relationship with God… it does not feel foreign.

It feels familiar.

Becoming Mothers Who Can Hold Both

This is the stretch.

To be:

- strong, but soft
- guiding, but listening
- leading, but not controlling
- present, but not possessive

To raise children who:

- think
- question
- grow
- wrestle
- and still feel safe coming home

To be proud of them…not because they reflect us perfectly, but because they are becoming fully.

Smarter. Stronger. More aware. More whole.

This Is What Healing Looks Like

Healing is not just:

"I'm doing better now."

Healing is:

"I parent differently now."

I listen more.
I control less.
I trust God more.
I trust what I planted.

And I am no longer raising children
to manage my fears.

I am raising them
to walk in their own identity.

What I Know Now

Children are not helpmates.

They are not emotional support systems.

They are not here to carry what we did not heal.

They need:

- direction
- covering
- presence
- love that is not rushed or divided

And yes, motherhood is hard. Yes, sometimes we do it while broken.

But we cannot build lives that require our children to heal us. That is not their role.

This Is the Ministry

If there is anything I will say without hesitation, it is this:

We cannot pray for children and abandon our own in the name of ministry. We cannot build the Kingdom while neglecting the first place God told us to steward. We cannot stand on platforms while our children are quietly asking for us at home.

That is not revival. That is imbalance.

And if we are honest… it is easier to minister to strangers than it is to be present with the ones who know us fully.

But God is not calling us to what is easier.

He is calling us to what is aligned.

Because the first ministry you will ever be entrusted with is not a microphone. It is not a title. It is not a platform. It is people.

And for many of us… it is the people in our home.

And I say this with both conviction and humility:

If my children do not experience the love of God through me first, then everything I say about Him publicly loses its weight.

Not because God is not real. But because I misrepresented Him.

And I refuse to continue to build a life where I am powerful in public and absent in private. That is not who God is forming me to be. And it is not the legacy I will leave.

Reflection Pause

Where have I confused calling with capacity?

_____

_____

_____

Where have I been present publicly but absent privately?

_____

_____

_____

What do I need to realign today?

_____

_____

_____

Where do I need to repent, not just adjust?

_____

_____

_____

A Prayer of Alignment

Lord,
bring my life back into order.

Teach me to recognize what is mine to carry
and what I have picked up out of pressure.

Heal the places where I have overextended
and undernurtured what You entrusted to me.

Help me to be present where it matters most.

Let my home not suffer
for the sake of what I am building outside of it.

And teach me to walk in a version of faithfulness
that reflects You fully.

Amen.

_____

_____

_____

_____

_____

_____

_____

_____

_____

_____

Selah

Pause here.

You are not called to be everything.

You are called to be aligned.

And that alignment…

begins at home.

Part Three - Ministry

Chapter 7

Leading With Love

When Protection Is Holy & Clarity is Kind

"Let all that you do be done in love."

— 1 Corinthians 16:14

I used to think leading with love meant slowing everything down.

Giving space.
Extending grace.
Holding room for process.
Listening longer.
Explaining more gently.
Waiting a little more.

And sometimes, it does mean that.

Love listens. Love waits.
Love absorbs. Love makes room.

But I have learned that love is not always slow.

Sometimes love moves quickly to protect what has been entrusted to it.

Love is patient in misunderstanding.
Love is gentle in weakness.
But love is decisive when harm is present.

That was a hard lesson for me, because for a long time, I thought the holiest leaders were the ones who could hold the most without flinching. The ones who could absorb tension, misunderstandings, personality conflict, dysfunction, and offense without ever letting it disturb the room. I thought love meant keeping things calm at all costs.

It does not.

To lead with love is not to avoid discomfort.
It is to act in alignment with truth, even when that action feels weighty.

Love without protection is sentiment.
Love with protection is stewardship.

Love Is Not Passivity

In ministry, love is often reduced to tone.

Be kind. Be soft. Be patient. Be accommodating.

And those are beautiful virtues. But tone without courage becomes passivity.

Leaders who confuse love with endless accommodation eventually burn out, not because they lacked compassion, but because they lacked clarity. They begin to tolerate what should have been addressed, delay what should have been resolved, and spiritualize what is actually misalignment.

Love does not mean absorbing dysfunction, so others remain comfortable.

Love means telling the truth when it would be easier to stay silent.
Love means correcting when it would be easier to overlook.
Love means enforcing what has already been agreed upon.
Love means protecting people, not just preserving appearances.

If love never requires courage, it is not fully love.

Some of the most damaging things I have seen in leadership were not done by cruel people. They were done by conflict-avoidant people. By leaders who wanted peace so badly that they delayed truth. By people who mistook patience for indefinite postponement. By good-hearted leaders who kept hoping something would resolve itself if they just prayed a little more, waited a little longer, softened a little further.

But unaddressed misalignment does not become harmless with time.

It becomes culture.

I did not learn this from theory.
I learned this from misalignment.
From moments where I delayed what I already knew was right.
From situations where I chose comfort over clarity, and paid for it later.

This is not philosophy for me.
It is correction.

The Weight of Loving Well

Loving well in leadership is costly.

It requires discernment.

There are moments that require patience.
There are moments that require confrontation.
There are moments that require space.
And there are moments that require structure.

The mistake is not in choosing gentleness.
The mistake is in choosing gentleness when clarity is required.

Many leaders delay decisive action because they want to preserve relationships. They do not want to disappoint people. They do not want to seem harsh. They do not want to rupture what feels precious.

I understand that instinct. I have lived it.

There have been moments in leadership where my heart wanted to preserve connection, but my spirit knew alignment had already been broken. Moments where the most loving thing was not to keep explaining, keep carrying, or keep accommodating, but to act. To respond. To choose integrity over comfort.

Because unresolved misalignment erodes relationships more slowly, and more permanently, than a single courageous conversation ever will.

Love is not measured by how long you delay.
It is measured by how faithfully you align.

Love and Authority

Authority without love becomes control.
Love without authority becomes chaos.

The healthiest leaders hold both.

Jesus embodied both.

He washed feet. He fed crowds. He restored dignity.
He touched the unclean and defended the vulnerable.

And He also rebuked hypocrisy.
Drove out corruption. Set boundaries. Walked away from crowds.
Refused to be manipulated by demand.

Softness and strength were never in conflict within Him.

To lead with love is to integrate both.

Not swinging between extremes.
Not reacting from emotion.
Not trying to preserve your image as either "nice" or "strong."

But responding from alignment.

For a long time, I think many of us, especially women in leadership,
have been quietly discipled into a distorted model of love. A model
where to be loving meant to be endlessly available. Endlessly
understanding. Endlessly absorbing. Endlessly patient, even when
patience had already stopped being virtuous and started becoming
enabling.

But love is not the absence of boundaries.
Love is strong enough to hold them.

When Love Costs You Relationships

There have been seasons in ministry when leading with love meant
walking away from people I loved deeply.

Not acquaintances. Not casual connections.
Friends who felt like family and walked with me though the heaviest of
my seasons.

We prayed together. We served together. We carried vision together.

And yet, there came a point when values diverged in ways I could not
reconcile without compromising convictions that are foundational to
my faith and to my own soul.

I did not walk away in anger.
I did not walk away in drama.
I did not walk away to protect reputation.

I walked away to protect alignment.

Because when integrity is preserved, ministry is safeguarded.
When integrity is compromised, everything begins to erode, quietly at first.

Walking away hurt.

It did not feel triumphant.
It felt quiet.
It felt like sitting in my car longer than necessary.
It felt like replaying conversations in my head.
It felt like grieving people who were still alive.

There is a loneliness that comes with choosing alignment when connection would have been easier.

And for someone who has survived abandonment, loneliness does not land neutrally.

It can stir old narratives and old fears. Old questions about whether choosing distance means losing love altogether. But I had to learn the difference between abandonment and alignment.

Abandonment is imposed. Alignment is chosen.

One strips you of safety. The other preserves your integrity.

That distinction mattered deeply to me.

I was not being abandoned. I was choosing clarity. And clarity, even when it narrows the room, does not remove God's covering.

Sometimes love is not expressed by staying.
Sometimes love is expressed by refusing to participate in what erodes integrity.

Preserving alignment preserved ministry. And sometimes that is the quiet cost of leading well.

Love is not fragile. Love is strong enough to hold boundaries. Love is not weakness. It is strength under control. And when love leads, people feel both seen and safe.

That is leadership. That is stewardship.

And that is the kind of leader I am still becoming.

When Love Requires You to Step Back

But I have also learned that love in leadership is not only about protecting ministry. It is about protecting order.

There was a season when I allowed the weight of ministry and the pull of duty to quietly overshadow my first assignment: my family.

The needs were constant.
The opportunities felt urgent.
The responsibility felt sacred.

And I convinced myself that sacrifice equaled faithfulness.

Rafael did not confront me harshly. He did not accuse.
He gently reminded me of something simple:

Ministry is an assignment. Marriage is a covenant. Motherhood is formation.

Assignments shift. Covenants endure.

Children do not need a mother who is applauded.
They need a mother who is present. That correction changed me.

Not because I stopped loving ministry.
But because I finally understood that love requires order.

I had to reframe the rhythm. God first. Family next. Church after. Not as a hierarchy of value, but as a rhythm of alignment. God is the source. Family is the first stewardship. Church is the overflow.

When that rhythm is intact, ministry flows from wholeness instead of depletion. When it is inverted, when church consumes what belongs to covenant, or calling overrides character, strain follows.

148

Love sometimes moves you forward.
Love sometimes pulls you home.

Both protect legacy.

There is a particular ache in realizing that good intentions can still create imbalance. I was not neglectful. I was devoted. But devotion without order can still wound what you love most.

Growth does not always come through confrontation.
Sometimes it comes through gentle correction from the person who knows you best.

And love receives that correction.

Love Is a Discipline

Leading with love is not a personality trait.

It is a discipline.

It requires:

- self-awareness
- emotional regulation
- theological clarity
- courage
- humility

It requires knowing when to slow down and when to step forward.

It requires refusing to weaponize Scripture.
It requires refusing to excuse harm.
It requires refusing to protect comfort over truth.

It requires the maturity to ask:
Am I trying to be liked? Or am I trying to be aligned? Because these are two different motives and every leader will face a moment when loving well costs them something.

Approval.
Comfort.

Perception.
Relationship.
Peace.

And in those moments, you must decide what kind of leader you are becoming.

Love is not the absence of tension.
It is the presence of integrity.

Sometimes the most loving thing you can do is say no.
Sometimes the most loving thing you can do is act quickly.
Sometimes the most loving thing you can do is draw a line, calmly, clearly, and without apology.

Love is not fragile. Love is strong enough to hold boundaries.

Love is not weakness. It is strength under control. And when love leads, people feel both seen and safe.

That is leadership.

Reflection Pause

Where have I mistaken love for passivity?

_____

_____

_____

What conversation have I delayed because I wanted to preserve comfort?

_____

_____

_____

Where do I need more courage, not less compassion?

_____

_____

_____

Is there a relationship, role, or responsibility that needs alignment instead of more accommodation?

_____

_____

_____

What would it look like to lead with both tenderness and truth?

_____

_____

_____

Write honestly. Leadership gets clearer when you stop editing your own discernment.

_____

_____

_____

A Prayer for Leaders

Lord,
teach me to lead with love that is both tender and clear.

Keep me from confusing softness with passivity
or courage with harshness.

Give me discernment to know when to wait
and when to act.

Help me protect what You have entrusted to me
without fear, pride, or performance.

Purify my motives.
Steady my voice.
Order my steps.

Make me the kind of leader
who does not hide behind tone,
but walks in truth with compassion.

Amen.

Selah

Pause here.

Love is not proven by how much you absorb.
It is revealed by how faithfully you protect what God entrusted to you.

_____

_____

_____

_____

_____

_____

Selah

Pause here.

Not to turn back.
But to recognize what you just chose.

Because choosing to become
is not just a decision.

It is a disruption.

Chapter 8

The Cost of Becoming

When Healing Disrupts Everything

"Behold, I am doing a new thing; now it springs forth, do you not perceive it?"
— Isaiah 43:19

Becoming sounds beautiful. At Least I hope it does to you.

It sounds like growth.
Like evolution.
Like stepping into purpose.
Like finally arriving at the version of yourself God always intended.

But what no one tells you is this: Becoming will cost you.

Not just comfort. Not just familiarity. But entire versions of your life that once felt normal.

Healing Is Not Gentle

We like to talk about healing like it is soft.

Like it is:

- candles
- journaling
- quiet reflection
- peaceful realizations

And sometimes it is.

But real healing? Real healing disrupts.

It confronts patterns. It exposes cycles.
It reveals what you tolerated. It pulls back the curtain on what you called normal but was never healthy.

Healing will make you:

- see differently
- respond differently
- require differently
- and refuse differently

And once you see… you cannot unsee.

You Will Outgrow People

This is one of the hardest truths to say out loud.

Not everyone will grow with you.

Some people were assigned to a version of you that no longer exists.

And when you change:

- your boundaries change
- your language changes
- your tolerance changes
- your availability changes

And suddenly, what once felt natural
starts to feel strained.

Not because you are better. Not because they are wrong.

But because you are no longer aligned. And alignment matters.

You Will Grieve What You Once Called Normal

Growth is not just gaining.

It is losing.

Losing:

- dynamics that once felt familiar
- relationships that once felt safe
- patterns that once felt predictable

Even if those things were not healthy. There is a grief in realizing:

"I cannot go back to who I was." Even if who you were felt easier. Even if it felt more accepted. Even if it required less of you.

The Loneliness No One Talks About

There is a specific kind of loneliness that comes with becoming.

Not because you are alone.
But because you are no longer fully at home
in spaces that once fit you perfectly.

You start to notice:

- conversations that feel shallow
- environments that feel misaligned
- expectations that no longer match who you are

And you cannot shrink back to make it fit again.

So you stand in the in-between.

Not who you were. Not fully surrounded by who you are becoming.

And that space?

It is holy.

Even when it feels uncomfortable.

There was a moment, quiet but undeniable, when I realized something had shifted in me permanently.

Nothing dramatic happened on the outside.
No explosion. No confrontation. No clear break.

But internally… everything felt different.

I was in a familiar space, around familiar people, in a rhythm that used to feel normal. And suddenly, it didn't.

The conversations felt surface-level.
The expectations felt misaligned.
The version of me that used to navigate that space effortlessly… wasn't there anymore.

And I remember thinking:

"I don't fit here the same way."

Not in arrogance. Not in judgment. Just in awareness.

And for a moment, I tried to adjust.

Tried to: soften what had become clear; ignore what I could now see; re-enter the version of myself that used to make everything flow

But I couldn't.

Because once God shows you something,
you don't have the luxury of pretending you don't see it anymore.

And that realization… was lonelier than I expected.

Not because I was rejected. But because I was no longer able to stay the same. That was the moment I understood:

Becoming is not just about stepping into something new.

It is about releasing what no longer fits… even when nothing about it is obviously wrong.

When Becoming Is Misinterpreted

There was a season, not a moment, but a stretch of time, where becoming cost me more than comfort.

It cost me perception.

For nearly two years, I found myself in spaces where I was:

- misunderstood
- questioned
- talked about
- and at times, quietly resisted

Not because I was out of alignment.But because I refused to shrink.

There were whispers. That I was too much.
Too strong.
Too direct.
Too visible.

That I carried a level of authority I had not "earned."
That I needed to soften, adjust, or step back to make others more comfortable.

And if I am honest, it would have been easier to do that.

To:

- tone it down
- make myself smaller
- become more palatable
- fit into expectations that felt safer for everyone else

But something in me knew:

If I shrink to be accepted,
I will lose the very thing God is trying to establish in me.

And that was not a price I was willing to pay.

The Discipline of Restraint

That season forced me into a different kind of strength.

Because I saw what was happening.

I felt it.

The misinterpretation. The quiet resistance.
The tension that sat just beneath the surface.

And everything in me wanted to explain.

To clarify.
To defend.
To make people understand me.

But God began to teach me something deeper:

Healing doesn't mean you stop noticing injustice.
It means you can see it clearly
without letting it consume you.

It means you recognize the wound
without reopening it.

Silence imposed is oppression.
Silence chosen is power.

I did not have to respond to everything I saw. I did not have to correct
every narrative. I did not have to prove my authority
to people who had already decided how they saw me. I could hold
truth without weaponizing it. I could honor my voice
without needing to use it in every moment. And that restraint… that
was new.

The Joseph Reality

God anchored something in me through the story of Joseph.

Because Joseph was not rejected for doing wrong. He was resisted
because he could see.

He carried vision. And vision has a way of exposing places where
others have stopped dreaming. That revelation shifted something in
me. Because I stopped personalizing everything. Not everyone who is
against you is actually fighting you.

Some are confronting something in themselves they have not healed.
Some are being reminded of dreams they abandoned.

And when you finally carry clarity, it can feel like confrontation to
those who have settled.

I Refused to Shrink

So I made a decision.

Not out of pride. Not out of defiance. But out of alignment.

I would not:

- dim my vision

- reduce my voice
- or trade my calling for approval

I would not make myself smaller to make someone else more comfortable. Because becoming requires courage. And courage is not loud. Sometimes it is quiet, steady, and unwavering. It is choosing to remain who you are even when it would be easier to become someone else.

When You Stop Performing

One of the biggest shifts in my life was this:

I stopped performing.

Not just publicly. Internally.

I stopped:

- over-explaining
- over-proving
- over-giving
- over-functioning

I stopped trying to earn belonging in spaces where I was already accepted by God. And that changed everything. Because performance is exhausting. And it will keep you trapped in versions of yourself that are sustainable for others… but not sustainable for you.

You Will Be Misunderstood

When you change, people will misunderstand you. They will say:

- "you've changed"
- "you're different"
- "you're not the same"

And they will be right. You are not.

But not all misunderstanding is injustice.

Sometimes it is evidence of growth.

You cannot evolve and remain fully recognizable to people who only knew the previous version of you.

You Will Question Yourself

Even when you are right. Even when you are aligned. Even when you know you are growing. You will still have moments where you ask:

Am I doing too much?
Am I becoming too much?
Am I losing something important?
Am I making the right decisions?

Because growth stretches identity.

And stretching can feel like instability
before it feels like strength.

But You Will Also Become Free

And this is the part that makes it worth it.

Freedom is alignment.

It is:

- knowing who you are
- knowing what you carry
- knowing what is yours
- and releasing what is not

Freedom is no longer negotiating your identity
to maintain connection. Freedom is no longer abandoning yourself
to keep peace. Freedom is standing fully in who you are
without apology. Dreamers do not need to defend themselves every
day. **Eventually, the dream speaks.**

I Am Still Becoming

I have not figured this out fully. I am not writing from arrival. I am writing from awareness. From process. From tension. From real-time refinement.

There are still areas where I am growing. Still places where God is stretching me. Still moments where I have to choose alignment again. And that is the beauty of this whole journey. We are not called to perfection. We are called to becoming.

This Is What It Costs

Becoming will cost you:

- comfort
- predictability
- approval
- proximity
- and sometimes even identity as you knew it

But what you gain?

Clarity.
Alignment.
Peace.
Freedom.
Wholeness.

And a life that actually reflects who you are becoming.

Reflection Pause

What am I outgrowing right now?

_____

_____

_____

What feels misaligned that I have been avoiding?

_____

_____

_____

Where am I being invited to grow, even if it feels uncomfortable?

_____

_____

_____

What am I afraid to release? What version of me am I trying to hold onto that God is asking me to surrender?

_____

_____

_____

A Prayer for Becoming

Lord,
give me the courage to become
without shrinking back into what is familiar.

Help me release what I have outgrown
without bitterness or fear.

Strengthen me in the in-between
where I am no longer who I was
but not fully settled into who I am becoming.

Teach me to trust You in the stretching.

And remind me that growth
is not loss…
it is transformation.

Amen.

_____

_____

_____

_____

_____

_____

_____

_____

_____

_____

Selah

Pause here.

Becoming is not easy.
But it is holy.

And you are allowed to grow
even if it changes everything.

Chapter 9

I Chose All of It
Becoming Without Fragmenting

"I will praise You, for I am fearfully and wonderfully made."

— Psalm 139:14

There was a time when I thought I had to choose.

Choose between:

- motherhood or ministry
- calling or career
- faith or ambition
- structure or softness
- survival or dreaming

Choose which version of myself would be acceptable.
Choose which parts of me could come forward.
Choose which parts needed to stay hidden so I could be taken seriously.

So I learned how to fragment.

I learned how to:

- show up one way at church
- another way at work
- another way at home
- another way in pain
- another way in strength

And for a while, it worked.

I was effective.
I was respected.
I was building.
I was moving.

But I was also divided. Because fragmentation will help you function…
but it will not let you become.

The Lie I Had to Unlearn

Somewhere along the way, I believed something that sounded
spiritual… but wasn't.

That God belonged in certain spaces more than others.

That He was:

- more present in the sanctuary than in the boardroom
- more present in prayer than in strategy
- more present in worship than in work
- more present in ministry than in motherhood

But that is not truth. That is limitation. Because the same God who meets you at the altar is the same God who meets you in your decisions.

In your work.
In your leadership.
In your business.
In your home.
In your creativity.
In your rest.

There is no divide. There is only awareness.

I Stopped Separating Myself

Healing did not just teach me how to love better.

It taught me how to live whole.

To stop segmenting my life into categories that made sense to people but disconnected me from myself.

There is:

- God in my motherhood
- God in my marriage
- God in my leadership
- God in my business
- God in my creativity
- God in my rest
- God in my voice

Not in pieces. All of it.

And I had to come to a place where I stopped asking:

"Which version of me is acceptable here?"

And started asking:

"Can I be fully who God created me to be... everywhere?"

The Story I Haven't Told Yet

There is a part of this story I have not written yet.

Not because it doesn't matter. Not because it isn't true.
But because I am still honoring the timing of it.

There are moments... experiences... realities... that shaped this version of me in ways that cannot be reduced to a paragraph. It took more than growth to get here.

It took breaking.
It took pressure.
It took moments that felt like they would undo me completely.

There was a kind of violence to my becoming.

Not always physical. But real.

The kind that strips you. Confronts you. Refines you. Forces you to face what you would rather avoid. And most people will never see that part.

They will chose to only see:

- the clarity
- the strength
- the voice
- the confidence
- the life that looks whole

But they will ignore or choose to not see the sandpaper.

The friction. The refining. The quiet decisions to become someone different when everything in me wanted to stay the same.

There is a story behind this version of me.

A full one.

And I will tell it.

Just not here.

Not yet.

Because some testimonies are not withheld out of fear. They are stewarded with wisdom.mWhat I will say is this:

I did not arrive here untouched.

I arrived here transformed.

I No Longer Need to Be Understood

There was a time when I needed to be understood.

To be explained correctly.
To be seen accurately.
To be received without distortion.

But becoming has taught me something freeing:

I do not need to be fully understood
to be fully aligned.

And that changed the way I move.

I Chose This Life

This is the part I want to say clearly:

I chose this.

But I need to tell the truth alongside that.

There was a time when I did not feel like I had a choice.

I was a victim of circumstances. Of trauma. Of pain I did not create, but still had to carry.

There were seasons where I was not choosing freely…
I was surviving. Responding. Adapting. Trying to make sense of what had already been set in motion around me. And survival does not always feel like choice.

It feels like necessity.

So no, I did not always feel empowered.
I did not always feel in control.
I did not always feel like I was building something intentional.

But somewhere along the way… something shifted. Healing gave me back what trauma tried to take from me:

Choice.

Not perfect control. Not easy decisions. But the ability to decide who I would becomein spite of what I had been through.

And from that place—

I chose this.

Not accidentally. Not passively. Not because it was easy.

I chose:

- to serve God
- to pursue my wildest dreams
- to build
- to write
- to lead
- to mother
- to love
- to become

I chose to be the author my Mami dreamed of becoming. I chose to step into spaces that once intimidated me. I chose to believe that my voice matters— not because it is perfect, but because it is mine.

And I chose to stop shrinking so that other people could feel more comfortable around me.

The Courage That Held Me

If I am honest, I did not arrive here alone.

Rafael created a safety in my life
that allowed courage to grow without fear of collapse.

My children showed me what it looks like to:

- question
- explore
- become
- evolve
- and still remain rooted

They did not perform identity. They lived it. And watching them gave me permission to do the same.

To be bold. To be honest. To be seen.

Not curated. Not filtered. Not reduced.

I Found My Voice

For a long time, I spoke in ways that were:

- acceptable
- palatable
- structured for approval

Even in ministry.
Even in leadership.
Even in spaces where I was technically "free."

But finding my voice was not about becoming louder.

It was about becoming aligned.

Aligned with:

- truth
- conviction
- identity
- and God

Now when I speak:

I am not trying to impress.
I am not trying to perform.
I am not trying to be received.

I am trying to be honest.

And honesty carries authority.

I See the Cloud

There is a moment in Scripture where a servant looks out and sees a cloud the size of a man's hand.

Small. Almost insignificant. Easy to overlook. But it was the signal. Rain was coming. And I feel that now. Not because everything is already fully formed. Not because every answer is clear. Not because every door is open.But because something has shifted.

Internally. Structurally. Spiritually. I see what God has been building. Not just around me… but within me.

And I know: What is coming will not look like what has been.

It will stretch.
It will expand.
It will require more.

But this time…

I am ready.

This Is the Life I Am Building

There was a time when I was not just navigating brokenness…

I was navigating lack.

Material lack.
Emotional lack.

Spiritual confusion that made me believe sacrifice always meant depletion.

I knew how to survive. I knew how to stretch.
I knew how to make something out of nothing.

But I did not always know how to live from abundance.

And part of my becoming was learning that God was not calling me to build a life rooted in constant lack. He was calling me to build something sustainable. Something whole.Something that did not require me to disappear to maintain it.

There is God in my business.

There is God in Levi Group.

There is God in how I lead as a People Ops executive.

There is God in the way I:

- host a table
- make coffee
- teach
- write
- build
- create
- and gather

There is God in The Levite Institute. There is God in every room I walk into.

Not because I am perfect. But because I am present. And I have stopped separating what God never divided.

I No Longer Have to Choose

This is the freedom.

I do not have to choose between:

- faith and ambition
- motherhood and calling

- leadership and softness
- structure and creativity

I can hold all of it. Not perfectly. But fully. Because God is not asking me to fragment. **He is asking me to integrate.**

Redemption Is Still Working

I cannot rewrite the moments I missed. I cannot go back and be who I did not yet know how to be. But I can be present now.

More aware. More intentional. More grounded.

And there is a grace in that. Because God does not only redeem outcomes. He redeems time.

And what I did not understand then…
I carry differently now.

I Chose All of It

I chose:

- the calling
- the process
- the stretching
- the healing
- the responsibility
- the visibility
- the cost

I chose to live a life where:

- God is not compartmentalized
- my identity is not fragmented
- and my voice is not silenced

I chose to become. And I am still choosing it. **Every day.**

Reflection Pause

Where am I still fragmenting myself?

_____

_____

_____

What part of my life have I separated from God?

_____

_____

_____

Where am I still trying to choose when God is asking me to integrate?

_____

_____

_____

What would it look like to live fully... without apology?

_____

_____

_____

A Prayer of Wholeness

Lord,
teach me to live whole.

Not divided.
Not fragmented.
Not performing.

Help me bring my full self
into every space You have called me to.

Align my life.
Strengthen my voice.
Ground my identity in You.

And give me the courage
to choose this life—fully and freely.

Amen.

_____

_____

_____

_____

_____

_____

_____

_____

_____

_____

Selah

Pause here.

Not because everything is finished.
But because something has shifted.

I am not who I was.

Not the version shaped only by survival.
Not the version that learned to carry everything
without ever being held.
Not the version that fragmented herself
just to make it through.

I have lived through love and loss.
Through marriage and breaking.
Through motherhood in its beauty and its weight.
Through ministry that stretched me
and seasons that almost undid me.

And somewhere in all of that...

I became.

Not all at once.
Not perfectly.
Not without cost.

But truly.

There are still parts of my story
that have not been written yet.

Not because they are hidden.
But because they are still unfolding.

I have learned that not everything
needs to be said all at once.

Some things are meant to be lived first.
Understood slowly.
Honored before they are shared.

And I trust that.

What I know now is this:

I no longer need to divide my life
to make it make sense.

I no longer need to shrink
to be received.

I no longer need to prove
what God has already established.

I can be:

A mother
A wife
A leader
A builder
A woman who loves God
and lives fully in the life He has given me

All at once.

I used to think becoming meant arriving.

Now I understand:

Becoming is staying.

Staying present.
Staying honest.
Staying open to growth.
Staying willing to be refined
without losing myself in the process.

And even now…

I am still becoming.

Still learning how to hold it all
without losing what matters most.

Still choosing alignment
when it would be easier to go back.

Still discovering
what it means to live whole.

If you are reading this
and you find yourself somewhere in the middle—

In the breaking
In the rebuilding
In the questions
In the quiet

You are not behind.

You are becoming.

And this?

This is not the end.

It is simply the place
where you realize
you are still writing your story.

Note from the Author

Before you go—don't slow down.

Go.

You've walked through pages that whispered, wrestled, and wept. You've stood in the tension between what was and what is still becoming.

And if you made it this far, something in you already shifted.

So don't go back.

All gas. No brakes.

Life is short.
And God does not wait for perfect conditions to refine the called.
He does it in the process.

In the middle.
In the tension.
In the becoming.

So move.

Keep your ear aligned.
Stay sensitive to His voice.
And make sure your yes… is still a yes.

Not to pressure.
Not to performance.
Not to fear.

But to God.

You don't need to have it all figured out.
You don't need to be fully healed to move forward.
You don't need permission to become.

You already said yes.

Now live like it.

Go build.
Go love.
Go lead.
Go mother.
Go write.
Go create.

Go live the life you prayed for
without apologizing for it.

This is your life.

All of it.

And you are allowed to walk in it
fully, boldly, and without division.

From my sacred mess to yours—
Now go.

You already said yes. Now live like it. The becoming doesn't wait.
Neither should you.

Maylene

About the Author

Maylene Peña (MAY-leen PE-nyuh) is a pastor, storyteller, and voice for the ones still becoming. She writes for the healers, the worshippers, and the weary, for those who carry both calling and chaos.

Known for her authenticity and spiritual insight, Maylene leads with compassion and candor. Her ministry and her writing invite others to see that God's love is not afraid of the mess but meets us right in it. Through her teaching and leadership, she helps others rediscover the beauty of vulnerability, the necessity of rest, and the holiness hidden in hard seasons.

Maylene is the founder of Levi Group LLC, where she equips leaders and organizations to build people-first cultures rooted in wholeness and grace. Her work bridges sacred truth and practical wisdom, helping others find the divine in the daily.

She is a Chicago native who currently lives in the Greater Chicago Area with her husband Rafael and their three children, Jelani, Jelise, and Jeliel, whose laughter and light continue to shape her faith. When she is not writing or teaching, Maylene can be found leading worship, mentoring emerging leaders, or finding God in ordinary moments.

She is the author of *Before the Mess Became Sacred* and *The Sacred Mess*, the first two books in a trilogy exploring healing, faith, and wholeness. Maylene believes that even in brokenness, beauty remains—and that grace is still the loudest sound in the room.

Made in the USA
Monee, IL
01 April 2026

46542022R00109